For Suzanne Desu

The ~ [barcode] S0-AVC-583 ~ ented
and sincere woman in all
the Napa Valley. —
Remember Camilles!

Saverali
9.3.10

The Gifts of Camillus

Celebrating the life of a Ministry

DISCLAIMERS

This book is designed to provide information in regard to the subject matter covered. It is sold with the understanding that the publisher and author are not engaged in rendering legal, accounting or other professional services. If such assistance is required, the services of competent professionals in these areas should be sought.

It is not the purpose of this book to reference all the available historical records, research findings and other information in the field of inquiry discussed here. Every effort has been made to make this book as accurate as possible, based on the published information available in the areas covered only up to the printing date. However, there **may be mistakes** both typographical and in content.

The purpose of this book is to inform persons interested in the areas of the history of the Congregation of the Little Brothers of the Good Shepherd and Camillus House. The Institute of Homeless Studies Press and the author shall have neither liability nor responsibility to any person or entity with respect to any loss or damage caused, or alleged to be caused, directly or indirectly by the information contained in this book.

If you do not wish to be bound by the above, you may return this book to the publisher for a full refund.

The Gifts of Camillus

Celebrating the life of a Ministry

Paul R. Ahr, Ph.D.

INSTITUTE OF
HOMELESS
STUDIES PRESS

The Gifts of Camillus: *Celebrating the life of a Ministry*

Copyright © 2010 by Camillus House, Inc.

All rights reserved. No part of this book may be reproduced or transmitted in any form or by any means, electronic or mechanical, including photocopying, recording or by any information storage and retrieval system without written permission from the publisher, except for the inclusion of quotations in a review.

Published by:

 INSTITUTE OF
HOMELESS
STUDIES PRESS

Institute of Homeless Studies Press
336 NW 5th Street
Miami, Florida 33128

D10473M

Printed in the United States of America

ISBN: 978-0-9817243-2-4

Library of Congress Control Number: 2010928618

About the Cover:

This painting by Patricia A. Forde, titled *Through the Heart of Camillus*, was first requested for another book about the life of the Camillus organization. However, as *The Gifts of Camillus* evolved, I became more and more convinced that it was best used here.

As *Through the Heart of Camillus* aptly symbolizes, Camillus House is a place of transformation for our guests and clients.

Where they experience fear, we offer hope with the gift of our kindness.
Where they experience shame, we offer dignity with the gift of our respect.
Where they experience hurt, we offer healing with the gift of compassion.
Where they experience isolation, we offer community with the gift of our acceptance.

These gifts of *kindness, respect, compassion* and *acceptance* are freely given by the Brothers, volunteers and staff of Camillus in accordance with the charisms of the Brothers of the Good Shepherd of respect for human dignity, availability, hospitality, flexibility and adaptability.

ACKNOWLEDGMENTS

For 50 years the Brothers of the Good Shepherd in Miami have provided positive role models to all associated with their Ministry at Camillus House. I have had the privilege to work alongside several of the Brothers, including Brother Mateo Fenza, BGS, Brother Majella Marchand, BGS, Brother Raphael Mieszala, BGS, Brother Richard Moore, BGS, Brother Bill Osmanski, BGS, and Brother Charles Searson, BGS. I have also benefited from the leadership of two wonderful Brothers General of the Congregation: Brother David Lynch, BGS and Brother Justin Howson, BGS. Thanks to these men and all of the members of the Congregation for their unselfish gift of service to persons who are poor and homeless in Miami and for their inspiration to me.

Throughout my tenure as president and CEO of Camillus House, I have been honored to work for and with one extraordinary Chairman of the Board, Mr. Bob Dickinson. I have also had the privilege to work with our *Chairman Emeritus*, Mr. Roger D. Soman, who passed away earlier this year. Persons who are poor and homeless in Miami have had no greater champions than Bob Dickinson and Roger Soman, and I salute them both. Roger, we miss you already.

Paul Johnson, who was Camillus CEO in the 1980s and 1990s, challenged me to use the vehicles of these *Letters* to present to the general readership the experience of being homeless from the perspective of homeless persons themselves. I hope that the 2009 Letters, *This Is What We Do: Reflections on the experience of being homeless in Miami* comes close to what he had in mind.

Since the release of *Letters to Camillus*, I have had the great fortune to complete the *International Program in Spirituality Studies* at St. Thomas University's School of Theology and Ministry under the guidance of Ms. Ann Rose. This life-changing spirituality-enriching experience has helped me better understand the *good news* of the Brothers' Ministry in Miami, and better appreciate the *goodness* of my friend and role model, Jack Lally of St. Louis.

Special thanks go again to my wife, Patricia A. Forde, for serving both as a gentle critic of my writing, and as a compassionate companion in our love for the persons Camillus serves. Her dedication to the work of Camillus House and Camillus Health Concern is beautifully portrayed in her painting, *Through the Heart of Camillus,* which is presented on the cover of this book.

Patricia Cawley, Karen Mahar and Brother Raphael Mieszala, BGS were always ready with constructive feedback and valuable background information as was Sam Gil, who doubled as editor and publisher of this book. Once again, Sam, Brother Raphael and I were assisted in our research by the gracious help of Wm. Kevin Cawley, Archivist and Curator of Manuscripts, and the staff at the University of Notre Dame's Hesburgh Library Archives. Thanks also to Professor Pedro A. Figueredo and the staff at the Archbishop John C. Favalora Archive and Museum at St. Thomas University for their assistance. Beth and Bob Sackstein generously shared photographs from their personal collecion for this book.

Barb and Jim Weems of *Ad Graphics* have once again performed their magic, transforming thousands of words and images into this beautiful little book.

Finally, thanks to all the benefactors, volunteers and staff of Camillus House and Camillus Health Concern for transforming homelessness into hopefulness for thousands of persons in Miami-Dade County, Florida.

CONTENTS

FOREWORD

For 50 years, the Brothers of the Good Shepherd and dedicated staff and volunteers have carried out the pledge of *charity unlimited* first given in 1960 by our founder, Brother Mathias Barrett, BGS to those who are poor and homeless in Miami. True to this promise, the wonderful men and women who have served alongside the Brothers – whether as Board members, other volunteers or staff – have created Camillus House and Camillus Health Concern (Camillus) as a caring family for those persons who are most vulnerable in South Florida. *The Gifts of Camillus: Celebrating the life of a Ministry*, serves as an album – our family album – in which various contributions of the Camillus family and our overarching Catholic Christian traditions are collected and displayed.

The special role that the Camillus organization plays in the South Florida community can be best understood in terms of the five charisms of the Brothers of the Good Shepherd: availability, hospitality, flexibility, adaptability and respect for human dignity. In the section, *Camillus' Ministry in South Florida: Fifty years of service to our neighbors who are poor and homeless*, Dr. Paul R. Ahr has succinctly summarized the ways in which the Camillus organization has applied these charisms as guideposts and tools to meet the evolving needs of those most in need in Miami.

The flexibility and adaptability of Camillus House leadership and staff continue to the present time and can be seen in such initiatives as the Camillus Courtyard and the construction of new facilities where persons who are poor and homeless will be greeted and served in the decades to come with the dignity that is theirs as daughters and sons of God, and thereby our sisters and brothers.

On behalf of the Congregation of the Brothers of the Good Shepherd, I want to express, once again, our thanks to Dr. Ahr and the staff of Camillus House and Camillus Health Concern for having such a compelling story to share with the South Florida community, and for sharing it in this personal way. Happy 50th Anniversary!

Brother Justin Howson, BGS
Brother General
Brothers of the Good Shepherd
June 1, 2010

INTRODUCTION

A plaque at the Camillus House Chapel of Divine Mercy commemorates in a brief prayer the founding of this great Ministry by Brother Mathias Barrett, BGS on August 20, 1960. This prayer reads in part:

Dear God, You sent us your humble servant Brother Mathias Barrett to tend to the needs of persons who are poor and sick and homeless in Miami. Brother Mathias so loved the people of Miami that he established Camillus House, a place of refuge and recovery to give witness to Your loving, healing and consoling power. The seed planted by Brother Mathias has grown into a tree of great height and reach, covering all who seek Your comfort and protection.

As we celebrate the 50th Anniversary of Brother Mathias' gift of Camillus to the people of South Florida, we call to mind the sacrifices of the Brothers of the Good Shepherd, the generous contributions of thousands of donors and volunteers and the unwavering dedication of Camillus House and Camillus Health Concern staff that have nurtured the seed planted by our founder.

This year we planted new seeds as we began construction on two new Camillus House facilities. One is Labre Place, a 90-unit apartment building near Downtown Miami for persons who are homeless. The second is the New Camillus House Campus, a complex of emergency, transitional and permanent housing that will serve approximately 1,500 persons a year plus office, meeting and outpatient treatment spaces where non-residential homeless prevention, job readiness and substance abuse and mental health follow-up care programs annually will serve thousands more persons who are at-risk of being homeless or are homeless in South Florida.

I encourage all who read about what the Brothers of the Good Shepherd have given to the people of South Florida over the past 50 years to help us continue to build on the ongoing expansion of Camillus House and the good deeds of past and current Brothers, benefactors, volunteers and staff to assure that Camillus will continue helping those who are in need in our community for generations to come.

Bob Dickinson
Camillus House Board Chairman
Miami, Florida
May 31, 2010

PREFACE

Today, thanks to God, the Brothers of the Good Shepherd and the Board of Directors of Camillus House, I begin my seventh year as Camillus president and CEO. What started out as a short term assignment of 100 days, has progressed into a vocation twenty times that.

German Lutheran theologian Deitrich Bonhoeffer has written that "There is a meaning in every journey that is unknown to the traveler." Since 2004, I have learned that for the past 50 years, all of us, Brothers, Board members, benefactors, clients and guests have been on a journey together, a journey whose true meaning and meaningfulness we could not comprehend until we were well on our way. *The Gifts of Camillus: Celebrating the life of a Ministry*, is a scrapbook of the sights and sounds, successes and shortfalls along our way.

The Gifts of Camillus celebrates 50 years of service to the people of Miami-Dade County. Part 1 focuses on this outstanding history through the eyes of Miami Archbishop John C. Favalora, Brother General Justin Howson, BGS and Brothers of the Good Shepherd who served at Camillus House and Camillus Health Concern.

This Part also incorporates my 2010 "Letters." *Camillus' Ministry in South Florida: Fifty years of service to our neighbors who are poor and homeless* presents the unfolding of the Camillus mission in Miami – decade by decade – in the context of the changing faces of homelessness in South Florida and the nation. Finally, we have included some rarely seen photos of Camillus House and the Brothers, staff and volunteers who have worked here over the years.

Part 2 consists of my "Letters to Camillus" from 2005 through 2009, presented in the order of their publication. The attentive reader will note the changes in the services provided and the number of persons served during this period of time. Each set centers on a theme of importance to Camillus House as a Catholic Christian organization serving the needs of persons who are poor and homeless in Miami-Dade County, Florida.

2005: *Welcome Strangers & Friends: Reflections on Compassionate Hospitality* discusses the role of Camillus in providing hospitality to our neighbors who are poor and homeless.

2006: *Homeless But Not Hopeless: Reflections on being my brothers' and sisters' keeper* focuses on the relevance of the encyclicals of the late Pope John Paul II to the work of the Camillus organization.

2007: *The Journey Home: Rest stops on the road to our Father's house* reviews the ways in which the Sermon on the Mount is put into practice every day at Camillus.

2008: *I Was Poor and You Loved Me: The everyday practice of the Corporal Works of Mercy* focuses on the ways in which the Camillus organization carries out these important charitable acts in the service of others.

2009: *This Is What We Do: Reflections on the experience of being homeless in Miami* examines how the commitment of Camillus House to serve is experienced by persons who are and/or have been homeless.

Advent 2009: Hope, Dignity, Healing and Community presents a series of reflections prepared as we made ready the coming of the Camillus House Jubilee year.

Thank you, Brothers and benefactors for the gift of Camillus House!

Paul R. Ahr, Ph.D.
Miami Beach, Florida
April 29, 2010

PART
1

CHAPTER 1

Celebrating 50 Years of Service by the Brothers of the Good Shepherd

ARCHDIOCESE OF MIAMI
Office of the Archbishop

April 22, 2010

Dear Friends in Christ:

The Archdiocese of Miami, since its inception in 1958, has been enriched by so many blessings from Our Lord, almost too many to count.

Today I do want to count the blessings that came to us when the Little Brothers of the Good Shepherd founded Camillus House at the invitation of our founding Archbishop, Coleman F. Carroll. Recognizing the growing presence of the poor among us, the Archbishop and the Brothers took up the challenge of the Lord Jesus' own preferential option for the poor.

The ever presence of the poor and homeless among us offer each of us the opportunity to see the face of Jesus and to minister to him daily. Our profession of love of God through love of neighbors takes on a special authenticity when we see the face of God daily in the poor and when the poor see God's face daily in the faces of so many who do the work of Camillus House.

Over these fifty years, thousands of supporters and volunteers have enabled Camillus House to be a place of welcome, a safe haven and sign of God's caring presence for those whose homes have become our urban streets and alley ways.

Camillus House is a blessing for the Archdiocese of Miami and for the City of Miami because we know that our clients are the Jesus, Mary and Joseph of today seeking food and shelter in their need. Thank God we have room. Thank God we have Camillus House and its many services of love.

Congratulations, Brothers. Congratulations, Dr. Ahr. Congratulations, honored Board members. Thank you, blessed supporters of Camillus House. May you see God.

Sincerely in the Lord,

John C. Favalora

Archbishop of Miami

Celebrating 50 Years of Service in Miami

Remarks delivered by Brother Justin Howson, BGS, Brother General at the Mass and candlelight service commemorating the Camillus House Jubilee Year, January 19, 2010

Having lived with Brother Mathias, I can truly feel his presence among us. I can easily visualize him savoring every moment of this celebration.

He'd have sat upstairs in the front pew of this church, dressed in his tattered black suit or white religious habit, eyes closed, hands clasped together in prayerful gratitude, with that impish, characteristic smile that always expressed both his satisfaction and pleasure.

As the founder of the Little Brothers of the Good Shepherd and Camillus House, he'd be the star attraction here and as such, he'd surely be invited to "say a few words."

In his thick Irish brogue, I'm convinced that his message today would be simply this:

Never forget the poor and needy. Never, ever take them for granted. Remember that they are, warts and all, our brothers and sisters in need, hurting, mostly alone, often misunderstand and frequently shunned. Consider their humanity and treat them always with dignity and respect. Remember, an easy smile, a willing handshake, a sincere welcome builds trust.

He'd tell us from his experience that a hot cup of coffee and a decent meal helps break down the barriers between the giver and the receiver.

In all honesty, he'd remind us that the Ministry of Charity Unlimited – Never Stop Loving – the Ministry of Camillus House and Camillus House Health Concern, sounds and looks romantically easy and appealing to many, but that, in fact, it is mostly frustratingly difficult, complex, time-consuming and emotionally draining. We would be reminded that unless and until the Ministry is carried out with the *purest* of intentions, the poor, to quote St. Vincent de Paul, "will never forgive you for the good you do them." The poor have feelings too!

Then, he would turn his attention to the past 50 years, to the hard work done by the founding Brothers, staff members and volunteers. He would recognize the tenacious perseverance under mostly difficult circumstances of the Brothers, directors, and CEOs, the many co-workers, volunteers and friends.

As only he could do, he would attribute thanks to the Board of Directors (past and present) and to the thousands of benefactors who have, down through the years, given freely and willingly, their financial support.

Somewhat afraid of government funding, he would understand its necessity and thank each funding agency accordingly.

Concerned with the practicalities of management, he would urge all parties involved to work through differences. An easy communicator, he'd recommend open and honest dialogue between leadership of the Brothers of the Good Shepherd and corporate management of Camillus House.

With interest, he would look at the development plans for Camillus House. Accustomed and familiar with small institutions and facilities, he would stress the need for accessibility, convenience and practicality.

He'd want the clients and the guests to find comfort and security within the walls of the new Camillus House. Especially, he would want the folks who will utilize both the buildings and the programs to find peace, hope and a renewed sense of self-worth. He'd want the guests and clients to know that Camillus House is a place that cares for them and believes in them. I know that he would be truly proud and supportive of all that is happening here in Miami.

And what of his Brothers? As a reluctant founder and never at a loss for words, he would simply advise us to be faithful and true to his dream of service to the poor and needy.

We would be encouraged to live out availability, hospitality, flexibility, adaptability and respect for human dignity.

Most important, we would be instructed to continue to be the bridge between the institutional Church and the people we serve.

He'd want us to always be ready and willing to change and adapt to unfolding and evolving needs – to learn from the past and be ready to face new challenges.

Assuredly, he would want us, his Brothers, to be that presence on site, that welcomes, supports and encourages!

He'd warn us to practice what we preach and to be faith-filled, men of action and compassion.

Lastly, with a devilish glint in his eyes and that impish smile, he'd say to all of us, "Thanks a lot. I'll pray for you tonight." Then he'd work the crowd, delighting and rejoicing in all that has been accomplished here in Miami.

Returning to Albuquerque, he'd give thanks to God and rest comfortably in the knowledge that the special people of Miami were being well served:

"Thanks a lot! Never lose faith and hope in the people you serve."

Before closing, I want to recognize Paul Johnson. As Brother Paul, he mostly carried, single-handedly, the weight of development, the pressures of fundraising and the stresses of administration. We are where we are today because of him and people like him.

Brother Mathias Barrett, BGS visits with an elderly man who is homeless in Miami.

Remarks of Paul R. Ahr, Ph.D.
Camillus House President and CEO
50th Anniversary Kick-Off Celebration
January 19, 2010

August 1960 was the middle of the long night of separation from country, family and friends for *los exiliados de Cuba.*

It was then that a small-framed Irishman came from Albuquerque to assist the Diocese of Miami address the physical, emotional and spiritual needs of the exiles congregating along the banks of the Biscayne Bay, mere blocks from here. In the midst of this darkness, Brother Mathias Barrett lit a candle that still burns brightly today. That candle is Camillus House.

Neither priest, nor politician nor potentate, this humble Brother of the Good Shepherd challenged, cajoled and convinced Bishops, Mayors and magnates to help him – and all of us – follow this simple call of the Gospels: *Whatever you do for these, the least of my brothers and sisters you do for Me.*

Neither priest, nor politician nor potentate, he was a story teller, dream weaver, and candle lighter, and today we – the Miami community – say to Brother Mathias and the Brothers of the Good Shepherd: thanks for coming to us, working with us and caring for us for the past 50 years.

In November 1962, upon learning of her death, Adlai Stevenson said of

Eleanor Roosevelt, "She would rather light a candle than curse the darkness and her glow has warmed the world."

Brothers of the Good Shepherd, for the past 50 years the glow generated by you and your predecessors has warmed this city and the worlds of thousands of men, women and children who have been poor and homeless in Miami.

Ladies and gentlemen, please join me is lighting your candles to commemorate the contributions of the Brothers of the Good Shepherd to our Miami community for the past 50 years. May your glow warm us as long as the poor are with us.

(From left to right): Brother David Lynch, BGS, Brother Richard MacPhee, BGS, Brother Justin Howson, BGS, and Brother Bill Osmanski, BGS celebrate the start of Camillus House's Golden Jubilee year with a Mass at Gesu Catholic Church in Downtown Miami on January 19, 2010.

Reflections on Camillus House
By Brother Raphael Mieszala, BGS

Barbara N (Barbie) was one of the best examples of why Camillus House exists. If the Camillus charism of "adaptability" had not been in place, it would have had to have been invented specifically for her. In Barbie alone, Camillus employees practiced most of the corporal works of mercy.

Barbie first presented herself to Camillus House through the women's shower program. After showering, she would put on one of her sequined cocktail dresses and 4-inch heels prior to pasting blue eye shadow across her forehead and bright red lipstick almost to her cheekbones. She was thin and aware that she wanted to "look nice."

Barbie did not accept anything more from Camillus until one day when she needed a bandage for a blister on her foot. That was a "breakthough" moment wherein she began to trust Rose Anderson, one of Camillus Health Concern's nurse practitioners.

One day, Rose asked me to visit Barbie in Jackson Memorial Hospital where she went for an evaluation. In the hospital, Barbie was diagnosed with abdominal cancer. Her doctor wanted to do surgery then start her on chemotherapy, both of which she refused. She told me she just wanted to go "home." When I asked where she lives, she said "near Camillus." I later learned that this meant sleeping on the sidewalk across the street from Camillus. Barbie seemed to be very uncomfortable in talking about her health or about being indoors. In any case, within days, Barbie slipped out of the hospital against medical advice.

Rose called me to help her look for Barbie and, as Rose had predicted, we found Barbie on the sidewalk near the shelter run by the Missionaries of Charity. We brought her to Camillus House but, in spite of our pleadings and promises, Barbie refused to go into the Camillus House courtyard or atrium. She said, "You can't trust those people." She only wanted to go into "an apartment." Meanwhile, the street would be her home.

Barbie's serious medical and psychological needs, coupled with her refusal to accept available help, prompted us to adapt our schedules and resources. We managed to get Barbie enrolled in Medicaid, start a bank account for her, and gather some clean clothes. Although her skin would be dark from mud, Barbie always had brightly painted lips and nails. She wore large chunky jewelry and loved the fur wrap we once found for her.

Visiting her on the street every day, I once decided to bring Barbie something special: a plateful of ham, sweet potatoes, asparagus and dessert along with a can of grape juice. When I woke her up, she looked at me and said, "Where have you been? I've been waiting for you." As usual, she held up her hand for me to kiss (which I did). Then I apologized for being late (even though I was never regular in my visiting times).

After some weeks, a furnished one-bedroom apartment became available at Somerville Housing, a 48-unit housing complex built and run by Camillus for homeless people transitioning to a normal lifestyle. Barbie was so happy and moved in without complaint. By this time, Barbie was slowing down in her walking. While she didn't complain of much pain, Barbie had a hard time getting out of bed. Her cancer was making it difficult for her to eat or to control her functions. Brother Bill was heroic in changing her sheets and scrubbing the floor to clean up the trail made by Barbie as she struggled to get to the bathroom on time. Finally, on the 8th day of living in her new apartment, the "Queen of the Silver Dollar" had gone to meet Our Lord . . . appropriately dressed in a frilly nightgown. Camillus House paid for Barbie's cremation and burial. She now rests with many formerly homeless clients of Camillus.

Seeing Christ in the People we Serve
By Brother Bill Osmanski, BGS

I wish to highlight that beautiful passage in which Jesus spoke to His disciples about how important it is to surrender completely to serve the less fortunate. I speak of that moment when Jesus confirms His presence in the midst of suffering and says: "Whoever welcomes one child in my name welcomes me." Here Jesus used the example of this child to represent all those in society who do not count or do not have social standing such as the homeless, orphans, handicapped both physical and mental who suffer and have not been consoled.

We must learn to see Christ especially in the faces of those with whom He Himself wished to be indentified… "I was hungry and you gave me food, I was thirsty and you game Me drink, I was a stranger and you visited Me, I was in prison and you came to Me."

The Brothers of the Good Shepherd take these exhortations of Jesus seriously in our daily ministries whatever they might be. Here in Miami, we can especially witness to God's merciful love with the many persons we encounter with so many urgent needs.

Personally, it has been my privilege, as it has for so many of our Brothers serving here over the last fifty years.

Memories of Camillus House
By Brother John Chenier, BGS

I was stationed at Camillus House from 1979 to 1989. I have many wonderful memories of the time I spent there.

The Brothers' residence was on the second floor above the dining room. Brother Paul Johnson was the Director. I remembered him having so much energy; he was always working well into the night. He had so many projects to be finished.

There were two elderly Brothers: Fred who was in his seventies, and Luke who was in his eighties. They helped wherever needed. We worked long hours.

It was a pleasure and a privilege to minister to the many people from Overtown. There were also refugees from Mexico, Cuba, Haiti and other countries. Some of the men had AIDS and we would keep them in the dormitory till they were admitted to the hospital.

My ministry was the gate ministry. We served two meals a day – morning and afternoon, where people would come in for nourishment. The dining room was so small that it could only accommodate 82 people at one time. I had to let people in when there was room. Sometimes, there were 400 to 500 people waiting under the hot sun or in the rain. On more than one occasion, one of them would come to my assistance when I was having trouble with a difficult client.

Being at the gate gave me an opportunity to get to know many of the people:

- *Maggie* who had a little son, Andrew. She would leave Andrew with us while she would go and pick tomatoes.
- *Rip* who helped me with the garden.
- *Kaumba* who drew a picture of a boy holding a baby goat in pencil. I still have it hanging in my room.
- *Geneve* who removed her top and arrived in the serving area to a stunned teacher with a group of students who were volunteering their time serving meals.
- *Paul Andre* who became homeless because he had AIDS. We cared for him till he was admitted to Jackson Memorial Hospital where he died.

Rose Anderson, a nurse who worked at Mercy Hospital, would volunteer in the evenings. We used the little office next to the front gate as a clinic.

I shall forever be grateful for the time I spent at Camillus House in Miami and for the many people who came into my life while I was there.

Happy 50th Anniversary, Camillus House!

My Time at Camillus House
By Brother Charles Searson, BGS

I first came to work at Camillus House in the fall of 2004. I was used to working with poor and homeless people at other facilities operated by the Brothers of the Good Shepherd but Camillus was a very different experience. Right from the start I became aware that the 'demand' for our various services – shelter, clothing, food, addiction program, counseling, etc. – was far greater than the 'supply', what we could offer. I also very soon noticed the great variety of backgrounds of our clients – a high proportion originating from other countries in the Caribbean, South America and beyond. Other special problems encountered in the Miami work included cramped and inadequate working conditions and frequent severe weather problems (e.g. extreme heat and humidity, flooding, hurricanes).

So the work here can be very busy and demanding. There is the frustration of constantly having to say "no" to people as our resources are stretched to the limit. There is the challenge of balancing rules (necessary to ensure fair and efficient service) against exceptions (to meet special needs). There is, however, always the satisfaction of knowing we are helping people to survive and maybe change their lives for the better. And we are aware that however hard things may be for the Brothers and staff, they are far worse for the homeless and needy men and women we are trying to help.

In my assigned job at the front window I found I was dealing with so many people each day I had to ration my time with each individual. As I got to know the clients better, I realized that they were a mixture: 'regulars' who had been coming to us for some time, maybe years; and new people, maybe seeking help for the first time in their lives. This made things easier to some extent – obviously I could deal more quickly with the 'regulars' and give more attention to the new people. But this approach also led to the danger of cynicism towards the 'regulars' and not taking them seriously (especially if they were difficult or demanding!). I came to realize that I had to take everybody seriously and listen sympathetically to them, even if I wasn't able to offer them anything tangible. Another lesson I had to learn was that, in dealing with so many people every day, I was bound to make mistakes.

Keeping the spiritual focus of our work helps avoid cynicism and lack of compassion in dealing with the pressures. Reminding myself of Jesus' particular concern for society's outcasts and recent Church documents' emphasis on the 'preferential option for the poor,' I can more easily sympathize with the poor person in front of me. Other reminders of spiritual realities come obviously from our weekly Mass in the Divine Mercy chapel and, maybe less obviously, in almost daily expressions of faith and trust in God from our clients.

In my time at Camillus House I've seen many changes. As well as the inevitable turnover of staff and volunteers, changes of office, redecorations etc., there have been frequent changes to our services and procedures. We always have to adapt to meet changing needs. So, for example, when I first arrived, overnight shelter beds were assigned from the front office, usually in the morning; later they were assigned in the atrium in the afternoon. Once they were assigned on a night-by-night basis, with a limited number of nights allowed; later they were assigned on a week-by-week basis. Currently the shelter operates almost like a program: men (and now even a few women!) are admitted to stay as vacancies arise, are assigned case managers and stay as long as they need. When I first came, only 25 – 30 beds were available for the overnight shelter, now an additional 140 individuals can be admitted, although they have to sleep on mats laid down in the dining room and covered courtyard. Meal times have changed too: we now provide a lunch between 11 and 12, and the timing of our main meal has shifted from mid-afternoon to evening. If to live is to change, there has been a lot of life in Camillus House in the last few years!

Another noticeable feature of my time at Camillus House has been big things happening, special events and celebrations of various kinds. This has included 'scheduled' special events, such as the annual Thanksgiving dinner for our clients and the ISPA graduation ceremony; but also unusual events, such as the inauguration of the Brownsville Christian Housing project, the groundbreaking for the Labre Place apartment complex and, very important, the groundbreaking for the proposed new Camillus House on 7th Avenue. Recently, of course, there was the special Mass celebrated in Gesu Church as part of the celebrations for the 50th year since Brother Mathias started our work in Miami.

I have worked with some wonderful staff and volunteers who have often been an example to me. Our clients too have often impressed me with their courage in facing life when they have lost everything and their compassion. I always remember one afternoon when I was assigning beds in

"Doing Something...For Christ's Sake"
By Brother Majella Marchand, BGS

Christina came to the service window in Direct Services one day. "Brother Majella, can I ask you a question?" I responded with interest... Sure, Christina what is it? With a look of desperation mixed with determination she asked, "Do you love God?" Well Christina, I try to love Him with all my heart every day. "Well," she said, "for Christ's sake, do something!" I looked at her with concern and asked her, What do you mean, Christina? "Well for starters, we need soap, toilet tissue and feminine hygiene supplies in the ladies washroom. We haven't had these things available to us for days! Please help us!"

I assured her of my effort to get her list of items stocked as soon as we finished our conversation. We went on to share our thoughts about her additional concerns and she left the service window assured that her basic needs for personal hygiene would be provided.

After Christina left and things quieted down, I went back to make sure that all her requests were restocked. I asked the staff in Women's Services to reinforce their effort to insure that all these basic items were consistently stocked and they agreed to work with me on a day-to-day basis to make sure all these basic items would be readily available to our female clients through the day when they came into Camillus House for services.

At the end of the day, as I drove home to the Brothers residence, I meditated on the day's activities and thought about Christina's challenging question:

"[Majella] do you love God?" And, her pointed reply to my affirmative response by saying to me "for Christ's sake do something." I embraced the grace of her challenge by reaffirming my commitment to prove my love for God by making sure that I would do what I had been called to do by Him: to be a genuine presence and help to those who count on us for having their basic human needs met with the dignity, kindness and care they deserve.

That day, I came to better understand what the mission of Camillus House is meant to be. I realized that it must be more than just a dynamic of secular humanism. It has to be more than just a dynamic of social work. It can be – it **must** be – an honest response to an encounter with the living God, hidden and present in those who come to us for help. It must be a genuine response to provide service with a lively commitment to hospitality and respect for human dignity out of love for Him and it must never be an attitude that simply says that what we do is "good enough." The mission and Ministry of Camillus House is one that demonstrates availability and flexibility with a commitment of "doing something" out of love for God so that we can encounter Him, in the satisfied faces of every person we meet and serve through Camillus House activities. As I drove home at the end of that day, I thanked God for Christina's challenge to prove my love for Him by being and doing all I should be and do for everyone who comes to Camillus House for help.

Since then, I remind myself to "do something, for Christ's sake" with an expectation of finding God, real and ready to greet me in everyone I'll meet throughout my day. Christina was the agent that the Lord used to make my experience at Camillus House a reoccurring exercise in "finding God" in persons and events around me. And her voice continues to call me to do something, for Christ's sake! This wonderful experience with Christina has always kept me connected to what Camillus House should mean to the persons it serves! I hope it always remains faithful to this mission.

Reflections on Camillus House
By Brother Richard Moore, BGS

I was in Miami from November 2003 until January 2006. My day job was working in the front office referring clients to the different services that we have. One of these is the Institute of Social and Personal Adjustment (ISPA), which is a 60 bed nine month treatment program. Before that I worked at the warehouse as Director of Donations In-kind. However, strangely enough, hurricanes are my most prevalent memories of Miami. In the years 2004 and 2005 there were eight major hurricanes that had a landfall in the Miami area. There were actually twenty all told but in 2004 Charlie, Frances, Gaston and Ivan dropped by. In 2005 we had Dennis, Irene, Katrina (the most famous) and finally Wilma, the fastest and biggest.

By the time Wilma came around we had hurricane evacuation procedures down to an art form. The Brothers' job (mine anyway) was to escort and accompany all the ISPA clients to another location on the east side of the city to literally "weather the storm!" I can remember feeling distinctly nervous when I noticed the water at Biscayne Park lapping just below the sea wall like an over-filled bath tub.

By now, we had a good idea of what to expect, so all the preparations had been done: windows had been covered with corrugated iron, anything that could be brought inside was brought inside and anything that couldn't was tied down. Urns of coffee, trays of water, batteries, duct tape – all the essentials of survival – were moved from Camillus House along with 60 ISPA residents. We would literally "batten down the hatches" and wait for the storm. Matresses and bedrolls would be everywhere and one could hardly move for the bodies piled in the hallways.

At first we would follow the storm on TV but soon (when the storm hit the TV station) we would lose the reception. We would continue to follow it on the computer but then we would hear a crack of a wooden pylon [telephone pole] going down and so would the power. The next hour we would follow it on somebody's laptop and then, we didn't need to do little else, as we could hear the wind outside! By this time the whole building would be shaking in the darkness and a curfew was enforced so that we didn't lose anybody.

To pass the time, some of the clients, newly introduced to recovery, would start an impromptu AA/CA meeting. On more than one occasion I sat there shouting the Serenity Prayer or the Preamble trying to compete with a 175 mile-an-hour wind trying to rip the corrugated iron away from the windows. It seemed surreal to be sitting there in the dark, listening to somebody sharing their experience, strength and hope, while Mother Nature was busy trying to flatten the city. Mercifully the storm part of the Hurricane usually didn't take too long and by the morning we would be packing up ready to go back to Camillus House, survey the damage and clean up the mess.

Although the hurricane only took a matter of hours to pass through, it would often take days – and after Wilma weeks – for Miami Hydro [Florida Power & Light] to pass through and hook up our electricity again. I remember spending five weeks during October and November lining up behind a hundred of Miami's finest in the early hours of the morning desperate for a caffeine fix. I recall voluntarily working weekends at Camillus House because they still had power so I could get my laundry done and have my cell phone charged. My intake of current Hollywood movies shot up because there was still power on Miami Beach and I would watch movies instead of TV. Often I would come home with my heart thumping in my chest because a Hydro repair van sped past me and I'd be hoping that it was on the way to our house. I was usually wrong and would resign myself to another early night at eight o'clock in the evening with an iPod for company.

Due either to Murphy's Law or God's sense of humor (or both!) there hasn't been one hurricane touch down in Miami since I left. It was a privilege to witness all of this in the company of our guests in the ISPA program who had made that courageous decision to say YES to life and God's will and NO to self destruction and addiction.

I'll finish with a few short vignettes that come to mind when I think of Camillus House:

- Celebrating Christmas wearing shorts and a t-shirt
- Airboat trips in the Everglades throwing marshmallows at alligators
- Gelato at Coconut Grove
- Fundraising Galas on Carnival Cruise Line Ships
- Fundraising dinners at CHISPA
- Filling up containers for Haiti and Nicaragua at the warehouse

CHAPTER 2

Camillus' Ministry in South Florida

Reflections on fifty years of service to our neighbors who are poor and homeless

(Letters from the 2010 Lent Season)

50 Years in 40 days

Today is Ash Wednesday in Camillus House's Golden Jubilee Year. On August 20, 2010 we will celebrate the 50th Anniversary of our founding. This Lent my Letters will recount Camillus' history, one decade per week, ending with the Board of Directors' vision for the new Camillus House. Throughout, we will trace how, for 50 years, the charisms of the Brothers of the Good Shepherd – respect for human dignity, availability, hospitality, flexibility and adaptability – kept Camillus House related to and relevant for persons who are poor and homeless in Miami-Dade County.

A (very) short history of homelessness in America: 1770-1970.

The history in America of the phenomenon we refer to as homelessness is older than America itself. Colonial governments passed laws that restricted areas where poor transients could reside and/or required them to be indentured to settled families needing laborers. In the ensuing decades, social changes brought about by Civil War, large scale immigration, the shift from an agrarian to an industrial economy, and the Great Depression impacted on the numbers of homeless persons and how they were treated. Until the late 1940s, many displaced, transient or otherwise indigent persons (especially men) without a regular means of support found temporary housing in migrant camps (for seasonal agricultural work) and "skid row" districts in urban areas (for day labor at seaports and factories).

The post-war availability of affordable heavy equipment eliminated many low-wage urban jobs that required the combined strength of large numbers of able-bodied men, and soon that source of day labor income vanished.

Transient and otherwise indigent women who were not exploited and older persons who were poor and homeless were often provided for in County poor houses and State mental hospitals.

The 1950s and early 1960s in America – the formative years of the Congregation of the Little Brothers of the Good Shepherd (founded 1951) and Camillus House (founded 1960) – were marked by sustained economic growth. Despite the robustness of the overall economy, increasingly deteriorating core city "skid rows" remained the haunts of increasingly deteriorating poor persons, many, but not all, middle-aged and older primarily White men who were chronically alcoholic.

In Miami, this complex of social forces was enlarged by the influx of *exiliados Cubanos* fleeing tyranny in their home country. It was into this mix that Brother Mathias Barrett, BGS was invited to open what Miami Bishop Coleman Carroll called "Camillus House."

The changing face of homelessness: 1970-2010.

In the late 1960s through the 1980s, three social forces combined to change the face of homelessness in America. The first was economic. On the positive side, increases in Social Security benefits provided elderly persons who were poor a stable source of income to secure housing in low-income apartments. On the negative side, financial incentives to reclaim parts of core cities historically hosting "skid rows" of cheap single room occupancy boarding houses, hotels and restaurants led to the elimination of the only housing some abjectly poor persons could afford, forcing them to live on the streets or seek the hospitality of faith-based missions established nearby to serve them.

Secondly, beginning in the 1970s, persons traditionally served in public mental hospitals were discharged and/or diverted to community-based care that often lacked adequate housing and treatment supports. Many of them with serious mental illnesses joined the ranks of persons who are homeless. Finally, the availability of cheap and powerful illegal drugs brought a new scourge especially to many young but marginalized persons, and brought them to the ranks of the inner-city homeless.

Regrettably, the impact of illegal drugs did not discriminate on the basis of gender, race or age and the numbers of Black persons and women among the homeless population increased dramatically. By the end of the 1980s, the face of homelessness in America was a collage of male and female, Black and White, adult and children living with their families on the sidewalks, or on the streets in cars.

Social science research conducted in the 1980s documented the limitations of armory-style overnight shelters, and cities collaborated with the US Department of Housing and Urban Development to develop specialized transitional and permanent housing alternatives. The availability of affordable housing to persons and families who would otherwise be relegated to life of the streets began to reverse the trend, begun in the 1960s, of eliminating low cost housing. The pioneering activities of the late Alvah Chapman, Jr. and Alex Penelas propelled Miami-Dade County into the vanguard of communities embracing this model, a position it proudly retains.

Dr. Paul
February 17, 2010

Camillus House in the 1960s

> *"Camillus House"*
> *58 N.E. 8th St. Miami, Fla.*
> *25/8/60*
>
> *Dear Brother,*
> *Well, I am still going around, as this old house was found Monday. I moved in Tuesday, got water, light, gas and phone all going. Bishop gave it the name…The Bishop here wastes no time – but to get going- so it was the chance in a lifetime…I did write Brother David to come here…Best to all.*
>
> *Brother Mathias*

Writing from a rented seven room frame house, on August 25, 1960, Brother Mathias Barrett, BGS announced the creation of Camillus House in Miami on a 5¢ Air Mail Postal Card sent to his Congregation in Albuquerque, NM. Three months prior, on May 27, 1960, Brother Mathias was contacted by Monsignor James F. Enright who wrote that, "We have an urgent need in the Diocese for a home for Spanish speaking refugees, migrants and others who need some kind of a hostel until they can find work and a home."

On August 5, 1960, Brother Mathias was formally invited to come to Miami by Bishop Coleman Carroll to help meet the physical and spiritual needs of Cuban exiles congregating in the area now known as Bayfront Park near the Freedom Tower. "Please be assured of your welcome in the

Diocese of Miami," the Bishop wrote, "and if it will be possible for you to come to Miami, the nineteenth or twentieth of August, I shall be more than happy to see you." And come he did, memorializing their meeting in a letter to the Bishop dated September 7, 1960: "I will forever recall that 20th day of August 1960 when you said, 'Go ahead and get started this work for Christ's poor.'"

As if in a blink (or a twinkle) of an eye.

And just like that, the core mission of Camillus House of feeding, sheltering and rehabilitating persons who are indigent and homeless was set. "We are devoted to meeting the needs of the homeless men without work or families," Brother David Keane, BGS, Camillus's first permanent administrator, explained to the Miami *Herald*. "We offer a place to sleep, a friendly hand and meals."

The physical constraints of the frame house limited the hospitality of the Brothers to feeding the hungry and lodging a few men each night. At first, two meals were served each day, breakfast at 7 am and dinner at 4:30 pm. The dinner meal typically consisted of stew with bread and rolls. According to Brother David, to accommodate their predominantly Latin clientele, the Brothers liberally seasoned the stew with chili. Regardless of the background of the guest, the Brothers operated from the perspective that a full stomach improved the morale of hungry people, made them better able to deal with life's challenges and improved their chances of getting and keeping a job.

By 1963, the twice-daily meal program had been replaced by a hearty mid-day meal. In 1964, the Miami *Herald's* Kurt Luedtke described how the

Brothers approached feeding hungry Miamians: "To eat at Camillus House requires no repentance. There are no prayers, no sermons, no songs…All you have to do is stand in line with 1,000 men and women of many colors who cannot buy a meal." By the August 1965, Camillus had served more than 915,000 free meals.

A providential acquisition.

Within weeks of opening, the Brother's neighbors, the Rendells made their property around the corner at 728 N.E. 1st Avenue available to Camillus House on very favorable terms. The first floor store was converted into a kitchen and dining hall capable of feeding 600 persons a day. The dining room served its first meal on Christmas Day 1960. The second floor featured 13 furnished rooms and three baths, expanding the Brothers' ability to provide temporary lodging to men looking for work. Additional space also allowed for the Brothers to care for persons who were sick and elderly, and Brother Victor Nolan, BGS, a registered nurse, joined the Camillus staff. Brother David's focus on psychological and vocational rehabilitation and Brother Victor's expertise in health care established Camillus House's role as a healing as well as housing ministry within months of its inception, in contrast to a commonly held perception of Camillus House as "merely a soup kitchen."

Dr. Paul
February 25, 2010

Camillus House in the 1970s

The 1970s brought a continuing correspondence between then-Archbishop Coleman Carroll in Miami and Brother Mathias Barrett, BGS in Albuquerque. Their letters reflect a reciprocal fondness and respect, as well as a shared love for the poor. In a letter dated November 19, 1973, Brother Mathias wrote of his gratitude for the Archbishop's ongoing support for Camillus: "By the time you receive this letter you will have been to Camillus House and have served the poor men a lovely Thanksgiving dinner." He closed with thanks, "for all you do for us and for Christ's poor and now for all the dear Cuban refugees…"

A shelter for men who so badly need services.

The primary subject of their correspondence, though, was a shared desire for Camillus House to be expanded, "in the way you have in mind," Archbishop Carroll wrote to Brother Mathias in early 1973, "namely…a shelter for a limited number of the unfortunate old men who so badly need your services." In a letter to Archdiocesan Chancellor Monsignor Noel Fogarty, dated December 1975, Brother Mathias shared his frustration that this project – "a boarding house type of dwelling for those poor men who have difficulty in subsisting on a very meager pension and for some nothing at all" – was itself having difficulty getting underway.

A year later, the Archdiocesan newspaper, the *Voice*, carried this heartwarming headline: *Camillus addition planned to serve more of area poor*. Archbishop Carroll took this opportunity, the week before Christmas, to praise the work of the Brothers:

"As the Archdiocese is preparing its annual fund drive to assist those who cannot help themselves, we must also remember the work of the Brothers of the Good Shepherd. We must be reminded of the serious obligation to care for those less fortunate individuals," the archbishop continued.

"Many of them are without shelter; others barely have enough food on which to subsist each day. Then they find someone to whom they can turn for help – the good Brothers – who have for so many years accomplished this great work, which is indeed Christ's work. They minister to the poorest of the poor, to the homeless and downtrodden," Archbishop Carroll said.

On September 28, 1977, the Miami *Herald's* Barry Bearak told the rest of the story:

Tuesday afternoon [the Brothers of the Good Shepherd] held the blessing for the dormitory named for the late Archbishop Coleman Carroll at Camillus House...Archbishop Edward A. McCarthy officiated at the ceremony. Camillus House, a refuge for Miami's unfortunate, already has 15 beds and facilities for serving hundreds each day with hot meals. The new dorm, funded by $220,000 of private contributions, will raise sleeping capacity to 40.

"I remember when all we had was a bungalow," says Brother Mathias Barrett, 77, the man who opened the mission 17 years ago. "On the first night, one poor man came and I was able to give him corn flakes and milk."

New leadership and new challenges.

In November 1978, Brother Paul Johnson, BGS returned to Miami as Administrator of Camillus House, the first of several top management posts he would hold until 1998. Under his guidance, the Camillus organization would frame a comprehensive model of health care, employment and housing supports that would continue until today, and under his direction, the first steps to accomplish this visionary plan would come to fruition.

In December 2009, the Board of Directors of Camillus House honored Paul J. Johnson with the *Good Shepherd Award* for his two decades of service to persons who are poor and homeless in Miami. These sentiments were echoed at the Mass and Candlelight Ceremony that inaugurated the Camillus Jubilee Year in January, when Brother Justin Howson, BGS, the Congregation's Brother General, said of Paul Johnson's, tenure as Camillus CEO:

> Before closing I want to recognize Paul Johnson. As Brother Paul, he mostly carried, single-handedly, the weight of development, the pressures of fundraising and the stresses of administration. We are where we are today because of him and people like him.

Dr. Paul
March 4, 2010

Camillus House in the 1980s

Nationwide, the 1980s ushered in new challenges both for persons who were poor in America and the persons who served them. The public policy shifts ushered in with the new Administration in Washington led to less support for social and health programs at a time when the reduction in the size of public mental hospitals, the availability of inexpensive illegal drugs and the uptick in diseases like HIV/AIDS created growing numbers of persons without adequate resources to live a safe and dignified existence.

In Miami, the decade began with the influx of many, if not most, of the 125,000 Cuban refugees in the *Mariel Boatlift* that lasted from April to October 1980. For the better part of this decade, social problems experienced in all major cities in America were magnified in Miami by this international event and glamorized by the media through TV shows such as *Miami Vice*.

The emergence of competent and caring services for persons who are sick and addicted.

We have previously (February 28, 2008) recalled the contributions made by Dr. "Joe" Greer, Brother Paul Johnson as well as volunteers such as Rose Anderson, ARNP, Alina Perez-Stable, MSW and others in the establishment of Camillus Health Concern (CHC) in 1984. Begun as a voluntary humanitarian medical service by Jackson Memorial Hospital (JMH) residents, by January 1988 Camillus House had secured the building adjacent to the main dining room/dormitory facility and converted it, primarily through donated services, supplies and equipment, into a fully-functional medical clinic.

To the names of these pioneers should be added those of Beth Sackstein, JD who secured the Federal *McKinney Act* funds than underwrote the clinic expansion and other grants, and her husband, Dr. Robert Sackstein, a CHC volunteer from 1986-1992 who worked with Ira Clark, then JMH CEO and VA Medical Center Chief of Staff Dr. Eliseo Perez-Stable to establish critical working relationships with both institutions. Other volunteer physicians included Dr. George Ehringer, Dr. William Harrington, Jr. and Dr. Gwen Wurm. In 1989, psychologist Dr. Efraim Gonzalez inaugurated a volunteer mental health service.

Another treatment trailblazer came from within the ranks of the Brothers of the Good Shepherd. Brother Harry Somerville, BGS had been an educator prior to joining the Congregation. Recognizing the increasing and adverse impacts of illegal drugs on persons who were poor and homeless in Miami, in 1984 he established the Camillus House Addicts New Growth Experience (or C.H.A.N.G.E.) Group, a form of substance abuse treatment based on the Alcoholics Anonymous 12-step model. This program evolved into the state-licensed substance abuse and mental health treatment program later named the Camillus House Institute of Social and Personal Adjustment (CH-ISPA).

The neighborhood is changing.

As early as 1980, plans were being presented to redevelop the area described as Miami's "skid row" west of Biscayne Boulevard and at the north end of downtown Miami. According to the Miami *Herald's* Eric Rieder, this *New Town in Town* project was intended to "dramatically transform a crime ridden 86 acres…now occupied by flophouses, warehouses and a few businesses" – an area that included Camillus House – through the establishment of the Park West redevelopment district. One concrete product of this initiative was the construction of the *Miami Arena*, which opened in 1988, and was demolished 20 years later.

From the mid-1980s on, various strategies were proposed to purchase the Camillus House buildings on NE 1st Avenue and relocate its services, but none ever came to fruition. When some persons recommended condemning the Camillus property to clear the area and its clientele, cooler heads prevailed, led by City Commissioner Rosario Kennedy. Calls for relocation reached their peak as the opening day for the new *Arena* neared.

Simultaneously, Camillus was acquiring, through donation and purchase, the land on which CHC's Greer Building and both Camillus' Somerville Residence and the soon-to-be constructed Labre Place are located. In addition, Camillus purchased the building now known as Matt Talbot House to provide supervised aftercare living arrangements for working graduates of our substance abuse treatment programs, a function it still performs nearly 25 years later.

Against the backdrop of dramatic national, local and neighborhood changes, Camillus House prospered and grew through the 1980s, guided in great measure by an evolving vision of Camillus as a Ministry with a multi-site, multi-service mission – referred to as "The Camillus House Concept" – and an escalating appreciation of and respect by the community for the work of the Brothers in Miami and of Camillus' volunteers and staff.

Dr. Paul
March 11, 2010

Camillus House in the 1990s

If, as John Heywood first recorded in 1546, *it is an ill wind that blows no good*, then the storm that started modestly as a tropical wave off the western coast of Africa on August 14, 1992 was *not* an ill wind, although the residents of South Florida in that month would have likely disagreed. By August 24, that tropical wave had grown into Hurricane Andrew, crossing over South Florida with 150+ mph winds, causing 26 deaths (15 in Florida), ultimately destroying 600,000 homes and other structures, and leaving 200,000 persons homeless.

A community rebuilds.

In July 1992, Governor Lawton Chiles appointed Knight-Ridder Chairman and CEO Alvah H. Chapman, Jr. as Chairman of the first *Governor's Commission on Homeless*. The Commission was "charged with developing and beginning implementation of a strategic plan to serve the homeless in Dade County." Just as the *Commission* was getting underway, Hurricane Andrew changed both the nature of homelessness in Miami-Dade County, and the County's approach to it. Immediately, President George H. W. Bush and Governor Chiles invited Mr. Chapman to Chair *We Will Rebuild*, a civic response to the hurricane. By the end of 1992 a conceptual plan was developed and a dedicated public funding strategy was proposed in the form of a 1% sales tax on the sale of food and beverages in larger restaurants. The proposed tax was passed by the Florida Legislature with six minutes left in the 1993 session.

Before being levied, the new tax had to be approved by the newly expanded 13 member Miami-Dade County Commission. The state legislation called for the establishment of a task force to prepare an operational plan. Here Mr. Chapman was joined by Alex Penelas, then Chairman of the *County Commission Homeless Committee*. They and their colleagues on the *Homeless Task Force* propelled this County into the forefront of local governments solving the problems associated with ending homelessness. In addition to establishing the Miami-Dade County Homeless Trust (Homeless Trust) and the Miami-Dade County Homeless Plan, their successful efforts to secure the food and beverage tax made possible the construction and ongoing operations of the two Homeless Assistance Centers and made funds available for other new programs provided by community agencies. Today, the Homeless Trust partially supports 27 organizations participating in its *Continuum of Care*. While the wind that swept across Dade County in 1992 brought little, if any, good in the short term, it made possible great benefits in the long term.

Camillus expands.

Although Camillus House at first elected to forego applying for the new food and beverage tax funding, expansion continued in the 1990s. In 1993, Camillus acquired a cluster of single story apartments, on NW 77th Street for men completing addiction treatment. In 1997, primarily through the generosity of Dolores and Dr. Sanford Ziff, an atrium was added to the main shelter complex, providing rest rooms and a covered area where clients and guests, especially persons waiting to eat, could sit protected from the sun and rain.

Camillus Health Concern (CHC), the recipient of a US Department of Health and Human Services' Bureau of Primary Health Care *Health Care for the Homeless* grant since 1989, was designated as a *Federally Qualified*

Health Center in 1996. In June 1998, CHC moved into a new health center building, greatly increasing the number of patients served. In 1999, the CHC Board of Directors, first established in 1988, was reconstituted to meet Federal membership requirements. At that time the administration of CHC and Camillus House were also separated.

Finally, in June 1999 Camillus broke ground on its Somerville Residence on property adjacent to the new CHC building. Reporting on the event, the Miami *Herald's* Ana Acle interviewed Br. Raphael Mieszala, BGS, then Camillus president and Georgina Pardo, then president of the Downtown Miami Partnership. Both Brother Raphael and Ms. Pardo commented on the important role that the new 48 unit apartment building for families who were formerly homeless would play in the greater Miami-Dade community. According to Brother Raphael:

> We pray that by breaking the cycle of homelessness for residents of Somerville Apartments, the benefits… will resonate into the entire Miami-Dade community, as healthy families nurture healthy children who grow into contributing members of our community.

[This] "is not a downtown issue," Ms. Pardo pointed out, "it's a Dade County issue. There is a need for good quality, affordable housing." A decade later, the observations and sentiments of both these respondents would still ring true.

Dr. Paul
March 18, 2010

Camillus House in the 2000s

Camillus House entered the decade beginning on January 1, 2000 with a new clinic building, a main shelter that housed about 100 persons and two transitional living facilities with a combined capacity of less than 50 beds for graduates of its addictions treatment programs; all were situated north of downtown Miami. By December 31, 2009, that capacity grew more than seven-fold to 1,070, with the ability to expand to more than 1,200 in emergencies.

Filling a community need.

The single greatest increase in residential capacity came in the early 2000s when Camillus House was invited to take over first the management and then facilities of Metatherapy, Inc., a Homestead based not-for-profit agency. Once completed, this acquisition offered housing for approximately 400 men, women and children in the facilities now known as Brother Keily Place, Mother Seton Village, St. Michael's Residence and Beckham Hall as well as 40 persons at Brother Mathias Place an apartment-based program. Over the same time period, the Somerville Residence opened, providing housing for 150 men, women and children who were formerly homeless.

Later, 74 efficiency units for persons who were homeless were opened at the Brownsville Christian Housing Center, the former Christian Hospital which was the first hospital serving Miami's African-American community. Grants for up to 85 "scattered site" apartments were added, including the Archbishop Carroll Homes, an assertive community treatment program for formerly homeless persons with serious and persistent mental illnesses.

A plan to end chronic homelessness.

Three influences helped shape the contemporary focus of Camillus House. The first was the longstanding desire to relocate from the shelter site downtown, first expressed as the "Camillus House Concept" in the 1980s. The second was the setting of the goal of "ending chronic homeless in Miami," first articulated informally by the Camillus Board in 2002, and eventually operationalized in the Board's strategic plan which was adopted in January 2004. This plan provided a means to turn this aspiration into a reality, primarily through the addition of job training and placement programs and the systematic re-assignment of Camillus housing units to programs for persons who meet *both* the duration (homeless for a year or longer or 4 episodes of homelessness in 3 years) *and* disability (having a disabling physical, medical, psychiatric or addiction problem) conditions required to be designated as "chronically homeless." Grants for expanded substance abuse and mental illness programs added to the treatment arsenal.

Finally, changes in top management at Camillus House in early 2004 provided the opportunity to appoint to top leadership posts clinician-executives who, working within the plan, began de-coupling programs that served clients who did not meet the definition of chronic homelessness, and reassigning those resources to the advancement of the goal. While much still needs to be done to achieve total conversion to the agency primarily responsive to persons in Miami-Dade County who are chronically homeless, great strides have been made to date, and proposals are in place to accelerate this program redesign within the overall compassionate Ministry of the Brothers of the Good Shepherd.

The emergence of the Camillus Courtyard.

All good strategic plans carry within them guidance on how to respond to unique and/or unintended opportunities in ways that promote the overall goals of the organization, and the Board's 2004 plan met this test. In January 2007, efforts to discourage persons "camping out" in front of the Camillus main shelter by installing stadium-type lighting around the building resulted in an increase in "campers." In response, Camillus leadership invited our outside neighbors to come inside, allowing them to sleep in our parking lot. Drawn by the safety and hospitality offered by Camillus, this program, planned for 50-60 persons a night swelled to 280, most of whom had been habitually service resistant and many of whom were anti-social, seriously addicted and/or suffering from a chronic mental illness.

Now about 180 persons, most of whom have lived on the streets for more than 2 years, call the Camillus Courtyard home until they can – with the help of our comprehensive services – prepare for the next stop on their life journeys. Most will share the success of the 400+ former Courtyard guests who have left us over the past 2 years. Of these – most of whom were also once chronically homeless – 63% of the men and 84% of the women have moved successfully on to treatment and other residential settings as well as into independent living or been returned to family.

Dr. Paul
March 25, 2010

...to end chronic homelessness in Miami-Dade County in 10 years...

Success in achieving the Camillus House Board of Directors' goal to end chronic homelessness in Miami-Dade County within 10 years will depend on four factors: focus, flexibility, facilities and funding.

Focus: Persons who are poor and homeless in Miami have many needs, and the Camillus organization has a long and distinguished history of meeting these needs. However, in the five decades since its inception, nearly two dozen new agencies serving persons who are homeless have come on the scene in Miami-Dade County, allowing Camillus to further target its resources to those persons who have the greatest need. As the Camillus program has matured, some of the programs and facilities brought on line have became less appropriate for serving a clientele who are primarily chronically homeless. In response, management has been systematically redirecting funding and facility use to best serve persons who are chronically homeless, and new programs are being designed to serve this clientele.

Flexibility: Ending chronic homelessness is a complex problem that warrants a complex solution. Factors such as time on the street, resistance to intervention, level of severity and complexity of disabilities, citizenship status, and criminal background all converge to influence the readiness of a person to break his/her personal cycle of homelessness and the efficacy of plans that lead to a successful recovery and community reintegration. Guided by the Brothers' charisms of respect for human dignity, availability, hospitality, *adaptability and flexibility*, our clinical staff continue to develop progressively more complex solutions to respond to the challenges of progressively more complex cases.

Facilities: Three primary categories of settings will be required to carry out this plan. The first is a comprehensive reception/diagnosis/intervention facility that will both accept referrals from other agencies and welcome self-referrals by street-dwellers who choose to break the cycle of homelessness. This function will be performed by the main Camillus House program at our new site, where our Courtyard; Job Opportunity Bureau (J.O.B.) job readiness programs; and diagnosis, treatment and rehabilitation services of the Camillus Health Concern and the Institute of Social and Personal Adjustment (ISPA) will be expanded and better coordinated. Planned additions at this site will be substance abuse and mental illness services for women and for Spanish-speaking persons, and a Career Center.

The second category features transitional facilities for individuals preparing for/starting employment, undergoing treatment and/or participating in aftercare. Some needs are not being met and other needs will change as progress is made with less disabled, more responsive sub-groups of persons who are homeless. For example, a high priority unmet need is for a facility where addicted parents who are homeless can participate in treatment while keeping their families intact. Depending on the availability of funding, Camillus is especially well suited to offer such a program.

Finally, success will require the availability of additional permanent housing units, either through expansion of community-based housing (e.g., Brother Mathias apartments or the Carroll Homes "scattered site" apartments) or through new Camillus owned/operated apartments such as at the 80-unit Shepherd's Court on NW 7th Ave. and the 90-unit Labre Place on NW

4th St. Highest priority for these units will be reserved for homeless persons who are medically frail and/or who have disabling conditions that limit their ability to be economically self-sufficient.

Funding: Ending chronic homelessness in Miami-Dade County will require community support for both the construction and operation of our specialized programs. Financing has already been secured for the renovation of our Emmaus Place apartments for young men aging out of foster care, as well as for the Shepherd's Court and Labre Place apartments, both of which are scheduled to begin construction in May. At present levels of public and private sector commitments, our OPEN THE DOOR TO HOPE Capital Campaign continues to seek approximately $10 million to complete all phases of the new Camillus House campus development, including a modest endowment.

Ongoing support for our Courtyard, as well as for job readiness and for clinical treatment, will depend on private donations and a medley of federal, state and local governmental grants. Board members and staff, especially in our Offices of Strategy Management and Development, are dedicated to securing the resources needed to effectively build and operate the facilities and programs that will realize the goal of ending chronic homelessness in Miami.

We are grateful to all who have supported the Brothers of the Good Shepherd's Ministry in Miami these past 50 years and to all who will support our work in the months, years and decades to come.

Dr. Paul
April 1, 2010

CHAPTER 3

Photos

The first Brothers to join the order included, from left: Brother James Keily, Brother Kevin Carr, Brother Mathias Barrett, Brother Camillus Harbinson and Brother Francis Abraham.

Line of men waiting for a hot meal outside Camillus House shortly after Hurricane Donna.

Miami Bishop Coleman Carroll
(standing in an apron) serving food
at Camillus House.

Officers of the Miami Police
Department collected canned goods
for Camillus House.

Brother David Keane, BGS (left)
the first permanent director of
Camillus House is shown here with
volunteers in Homestead collecting
produce to be served to guests at
Camillus House.

A photo taken in 1960 of individuals having a meal at Camillus House.

Officers of the St. Vincent de Paul Society pledged their support by providing beds, blankets and other furnishings, as well as canned goods.

Folks from St. Michael's Parish and the Women's Guild help collect much needed goods to give to Camillus House in the early 1960s.

A group of men are shown here waiting to enter Camillus House in the 1960s.

Brother Paul Johnson, BGS (center) greets guests as they prepare to enter Camillus House in the1970s.

Men who were homeless in the 1970s are shown here enjoying a meal at Camillus House's dining room.

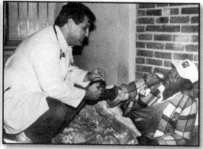

Dr. Pedro Jose Greer, Jr., co-founder of Camillus Health Concern, helps a man who is homeless in the 1980s.

Brother Harry Somerville, BGS, who established Camillus' first addiction program, speaks to a local Miami group about Camillus House in the 1980s.

Camillus Health Concern trailblazers (from left to right) Brother Patrick Collins, BGS, Beth Sackstein, Alina Perez-Stable, and Dr. Eliseo Perez-Stable.

(Photo: Beth and Bob Sackstein)

A Camillus client in the early 1990s stands next to the mural that formerly covered the shelter's Southern wall along NE 7th Street.

A staff member of Camillus Health Concern's Project Safestreet interviews a female client in the late 1990s near Camillus House.

Pat Cawley, LCSW, BCD a Camillus clinician, hosts a group meeting of clients in Camillus' treatment program, which was licensed by the State of Florida in 1997.

Staff and donors at the 1999 groundbreaking ceremony for the Somerville Residence, a 47-unit permanent housing program for formerly homeless families.

In 2000, Camillus House was invited to take over the management and facilities of Mete-therapy, Inc., a Homestead based not-for-profit agency. This acquisition expanded Camillus' housing capacity to accommodate an additional 400 individuals (men, women and children) in the facilities now known as Mother Seton Village (above left), Brother Keily Place (above right), St. Michael's Residence and Beckham Hall.

Ribbon cutting ceremony at the Brownsville Christian Housing Center, formerly the Christian Hospital, the first hospital serving Miami's African-American community and today it is a 74 efficiency-unit facility for persons who were homeless.

Dr. Kate M. Callahan, Chairwoman of the Camillus Health Concern Board of Directors presents the dedication plaque to Dr. Pedro Jose (Joe) Greer, Jr., naming CHC's medical facility (opened in 1997) the Greer Building in honor of his commitment to persons who are poor and homeless in Miami.

City, county and state officials joined developers and Camillus House to break ground on Labre Place, a 90-unit permanent housing facility for persons who are homeless set to open in 2011.

Bob Dickinson visits Camillus House clients at the main shelter facility.

Fred Mims (left) Director of Direct Care Ministry conducts a group session with Camillus clients.

Kathy Garcia (center) shares a jubilant moment with graduates of Camillus' Institute of Social and Personal Adjustment.

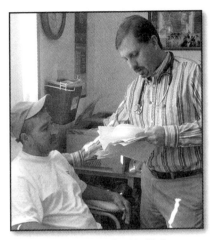

Dr. Javier Hiriart , Camillus Health Concern Chief Medical Officer, examines a patient.

Dr. Collazo shares a light moment with an elderly patient on a recent visit.

(Left to right) Alina Perez-Stable, former Executive Director of Camillus Health Concern and Hirut Kassaye, Executive Director of Camillus Health Concern.

City, county and state officials joined Camillus donors to break ground on the new Camillus House, a 340-bed campus designed to end chronic homelessness in Miami and set to open in 2012.

PART 2

CHAPTER 4

Welcome Strangers & Friends

Reflections on Compassionate Hospitality

(Letters from the 2005 Lent Season)

Dear Camillus House Board Members, Benefactors and Staff:

At the start of the 21st century, I believe that Miami is the best city in America in which to discuss the subject of compassionate hospitality. Here in the Miami area we have it all: a thriving hospitality industry (whose generosity to Camillus House is legendary); Universities that award degrees in hospitality and hospitality management; vibrant and vital cultures that provide hospitality to their own members and share their traditions with others; and an array of governmental, secular and faith-based organizations that do their best on behalf of others – often strangers – who need compassion, care and/or treatment.

During this Lenten season, I look forward to reflecting on, committing to writing and sharing with you thoughts on one of the core competencies of Camillus House: *compassionate hospitality* (the others being *comprehensive healing* with the Camillus Health Concern; and *community-based housing*). On Thursdays between February 17 and May 24, I will consider four hospitality themes.

1. Hospitality refers to the love of strangers.
2. The love of strangers (hospitality), especially the poor, is the love of God.
3. The strangers (our guests and clients) who come to us are pilgrims, each seeking a place to be safe before setting back out on his or her own personal journeys.

4. Hospitality always creates community, at least at the level of the host and the guest.

Along the way, I will introduce you to my personal guides, who include St. Benedict and St. Brigid, Jean Vanier, and the man who was my first psychology professor, Fr. Henri Nouwen. I hope that these reflections will promote a greater sense of community between and among us.

Over the weeks since our very successful Carnival *Valor* fundraiser, scores of persons who sailed with us have told me of the wonderful time they had that night. In *every* case, they listed at least one of the following reasons for their enjoyment of the experience.

1. The *Valor* crew did everything in their power to make it a refreshing and enjoyable experience.
2. The purpose for the event – to assist Camillus House's efforts to serve persons who are homeless – was so rewarding.
3. The event was an opportunity to be with old friends and make new acquaintances.

In short, hospitality on the Carnival *Valor* and at 726 N.E. 1st Avenue in Miami and at all the Camillus sites have much in common. Want more proof? Get to know Frank Ferrara, our new Food Service Manager. He has had very successful careers as a chef and as a restaurant manager (along with a career as a New York City policeman). Professionally and personally, Frank epitomizes the finest in hospitality. Since coming to Camillus House, Frank has transferred to his new calling all of his private sector dedication to attractive, nutritious and delicious food served amid exciting surroundings. Come to a meal at the 726 building. There you will see the fruits of the work of Frank, Miss Vida, Larry and some of the men in our program: flowers on the tables, tasty food that is attractive to look at and nutritious ("Sausage every morning?") Frank asks and answers his own question. "*Fugettabout* it; too many nitrates!" to eat. Frank is just one of our Camillus House staff who "get it" and share it – hospitality, that is. Over the next few weeks, I have the challenge to share our thoughts on hospitality with you.

Dr. Paul
February 9, 2005

Hospitality toward strangers is an ancient tradition, and may result in unexpectedly entertaining special guests.

This is the week when love is in the air. On Monday, lovers expressed their amour for each other through flowers, candy, trinkets and romantic dinners. Acquaintances and school children passed cards and candy hearts to commemorate the event. People of good cheer wear red to symbolize their affection for all they know; only the stranger is not included. Yet, the ancient Greek word for hospitality – *philoxenia* – means exactly that: love of strangers.

Hospitality among the Ancient Greeks.

When the shipwrecked Ulysses was awakened (likely on the island of Corfu) by the laughter of young women, he wondered whether the people of the land to which he had fled, "are cruel, and wild, and unjust, or do they love strangers and fear the gods?" [1] Happily, the hero was discovered by Nausicaa and her maidens, who took him to Alcinous, her father, where he was offered philoxenia, a supreme virtue in ancient Greece:

> Alcinous… took Ulysses by the hand… and bade him take the seat of Laodamas, who had been sitting beside him, and was his favorite son. A maid servant then brought him water in a beautiful golden ewer and poured it into a silver basin for him to wash his hands, and she drew a clean table beside him; an upper servant

brought him bread and offered him many good things of what there was in the house, and Ulysses ate and drank. Then Alcinous said to one of the servants, "Pontonous, mix a cup of wine and hand it round that we may make drink-offerings to Jove the lord of thunder, who is the protector of all well-disposed suppliants." [2]

Throughout his odyssey, Ulysses relies on the hospitality of others to return him to his homeland.

Hospitality in the Old Testament.

In Genesis 18:1-6, the stranger who received Abraham's hospitality was the Lord, Himself. Imagine the thirst and weariness of the strangers in the context of Miami's summer heat:

The Lord appeared to Abraham near the great trees of Mamre while he was sitting at the entrance to his tent in the heat of day. Abraham looked up and saw three men standing nearby. When he saw them, he hurried from the entrance of his tent to meet them and bowed low to the ground. He said, "If I have found favor in your eyes, my lord, do not pass your servant by. Let a little water be brought, and then you may all wash your feet and

Mother Teresa and Brother Paul Johnson serving meals at Camillus House.
(Source: Camillus House)

rest under this tree. Let me get you something to eat, so you can be refreshed and then go on your way – now that you have come to your servant."

"Very well," they answered, "do as you say." So Abraham hurried into the tent to Sarah. "Quick," he said, "get three seahs of fine flour and knead it and bake some bread." Then he ran into the herd and selected a choice tender calf and gave it to a servant, who hurried to prepare it. He then brought some curds and milk and the calf had been prepared, and set these before them. While they ate, he stood near them under a tree.

After enjoying Abraham's hospitality, the strangers proceeded on to Sodom (Genesis 19), where they encountered the hospitality of Lot:

...and Lot seeing them rose up to meet them, and he bowed himself with his face toward the ground, and he said, "Behold now, my lords, turn in, I pray you, into your servant's house, and tarry all night, and wash your feet, and you shall rise up early, and go on your ways." And they said, "No, but we will abide in the street all night." And he pressed upon them greatly, and they turned in unto him, and entered into his house, and he made them a feast and did bake unleavened bread, and they did eat.

Dr. Paul
February 17, 2005

For nearly 45 years, we have fed the hungry, given drink to the thirsty, clothed the naked, welcomed the stranger and treated the sick, one person at a time, often not knowing the identity of the stranger before us.

In the Book of Hebrews (13:2), we are advised, "Be not forgetful to entertain strangers, for thereby some have entertained angels unaware." Who might we entertain unaware? In Matthew 25:35-40, we learn that Christ may be the stranger, or, at least, that hospitality shown to a stranger is like hospitality shown to Him:

> For I was hungry and you gave me food, I was thirsty and you gave me drink, a stranger and you welcomed me, naked and you clothed me, ill and you cared for me, in prison and you visited me.' Then the righteous will answer him and say, 'Lord, when did we see you hungry and feed you, or thirsty and give you drink? When did we see you a stranger and welcome you, or naked and clothe you? When did we see you ill or in prison, and visit you?' And the king will say to them in reply, *'Amen, I say to you, whatever you did for one of these least brothers of mine, you did for me.'*

We are invited to use our special gifts when practicing hospitality.

When practicing hospitality, we are each encouraged to utilize the special gifts that we have been given:

Since we have gifts that differ according to the grace given to us, let us exercise them… Contribute to the needs of the holy ones; exercise hospitality… Rejoice with those who rejoice, weep with those who weep. Have the same regard with one another; do not be haughty but associate with the lowly… (Romans 12:14).

Or, as Peter wrote in his letter to the Christian communities in Asia Minor: "Be hospitable to one another without complaining. As each one has a gift, use it to serve one another as good stewards of God's varied grace" (1 Peter 4:10).

We are engaged in the group practice of hospitality.

Compassionate hospitality is an ongoing opportunity, not a once-in-a-while occurrence; it is an exercise, not an event. It is a way of life that requires discipline or practice (in fact, some versions of the Romans text above read: *practice* hospitality). It is as if all of us at Camillus House are in the *group practice of hospitality*, which we carry out by using or applying (or exercising)

A Camillus Volunteer helps a child.
(Photograph by Gina Fontana)

the differing gifts that each of us has been given to serve the least of our brothers and sisters. While we do these things because they are our calling, let us also be mindful of Christ's promise of a unique reward for acts of hospitality toward strangers: "Whoever receives you receives me and whoever receives me receives the one who sent me" (Matthew 10:40).

We intend to end chronic homelessness in Miami, one person at a time.

We are challenged to provide hospitality – to give food and drink, shelter and care – to each stranger who seeks our help. And that is how we intend to end chronic homelessness in this city: *one person at a time*. In conjunction with the other organizations dedicated to serving persons who are, have been or are at risk of becoming homeless, we will do it by providing compassionate hospitality, competent healing and a continuum of housing to one person who is homeless at a time. At Camillus House and Camillus Health Concern, we serve 1,000 free meals a day; house 800 persons a night; and we treat 300 persons with mental illness or chemical dependency and provide other life protecting medical and social services to more than 10,000 persons annually.

With the continued generosity of our benefactors, and the hoped-for opportunity to relocate to a larger building, we will be able to extend and expand our good works. And as we have done for nearly 45 years, we will continue to do these things, give food to the hungry and drink to the thirsty, clothes to the naked, shelter to the homeless, treatment to the sick, one person at a time, sometimes not knowing the identity of the stranger before us.

Dr. Paul
February 24, 2005

Homeless but not hopeless, our guests are pilgrims seeking our hospitality before setting out again on the journey of life.

From ancient times, the hospitality of individuals provided a safe refuge for persons who were traveling through strange or hostile areas. By the Middle Ages, these travelers – whether merchants, missionaries, pilgrims or soldiers – needed places for rest and refreshment along the way, and all, except the soldiers, also needed protection from highway robbers. It was in this context that monasteries opened their doors to travelers, especially pilgrims. In those days, hospitality was about safety, not about comfort.

Christian monasticism sprang up almost simultaneously in Egypt, Syria and Asia Minor at the beginning of the fourth century, coming to Western Europe about 430 A.D. The earliest monasteries were governed by local customs,

St. Benedict

typically established and enforced by the presiding abbot. One fourth century abbot who promulgated rules for the operation of his monastery was St. Macarius, whose *Rule* encouraged hospitality:

Pursuing hospitality in all things, do not avert your eye and abandon a pauper empty-handed, lest by chance the Lord come to you in a guest or in a pauper and see your hesitations, and you be condemned; but show yourself hospitable to all and act with faith.[3]

Benedictine hospitality toward pilgrims.

Over time, some compilations of rules gained more continuous or widespread use, the chief of these being the *Rule of St. Benedict*, promulgated by that abbot about 530 A.D. For St. Benedict, hospitality is openhanded; it is welcoming; it is up-close and personal. Hospitality is reciprocal: the host and guest represent Christ to each other. Benedictine hospitality is based on the principle that for me to be a whole person, I have to let others in. Thus, the host and guest require each other; in fact, the Indo-European root of both words host and guest are the same: *ghosti*.

One of the paradoxes of monastic hospitality was that the act of providing protection from danger introduced the possibility of danger actually entering the monastery itself, if the guest was a harmful person.

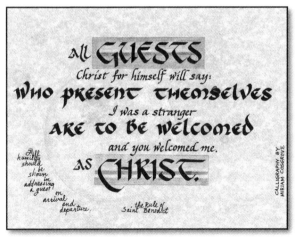

Chapter 53 Rule of St. Benedict

For St. Benedict, overcoming any discomfort or fear of strangers was handled by seeing Christ in all who presented themselves for safekeeping. In Chapter 53 of his *Holy Rule*, he set the standard for hospitality in Benedictine monasteries, echoing St. Macarius:

> Let all guests who arrive be received as Christ, because He will say: "I was a stranger and you took Me in. (Matthew 25:35-40)... Let the greatest care be taken, especially in the reception of the poor and travelers because Christ is received specially in them...

Many of Camilllus' clients have nowhere to turn.
(Photograph by Gina Fontana)

The *Rule of St. Benedict* set forth the arrangements to be made for the monastery's guests. Special courtesy was to be shown to the poor and the pilgrim, whose feet were to be washed by the abbot and the monks following the ancient custom, using Christ at the Last Supper as their model. Two monks were routinely on duty to prepare a meal at any hour for the guests and their host, the abbot; and sufficient beds and bedding were kept ready for those spending the night. Regardless of their reasons for seeking hospitality – whether to be nourished in body, mind, spirit or all – guests of the abbey were to be received and cherished as Christ.

We prepare to receive all who come to us, regardless of their reasons for being there.

I sometimes walk along NE 1st Avenue, engaging the persons standing, sitting and lying there. At those times I reflect on the relationship between Camillus House and the persons who live on the street in front of our shelter. I recognize each of them as a pilgrim, *homeless but not hopeless*, who relies on Camillus and the community that supports us to offer relief from hunger and disease and isolation and harm (whether inflicted by themselves or others); each person recovering in our midst before setting out again on life's journey. As we have done for nearly 45 years, Camillus House continuously prepares to receive them all – regardless of their reasons for seeking our hospitality.

Dr. Paul
March 3, 2005

Hospitality is the creation of a free and fearless space for people to be (or become) themselves.

In 1966, Henri Nouwen became my first psychology professor at the University of Notre Dame, and, alphabetically speaking, I was his first student. During the 30 years until his death, Fr. Nouwen became an internationally renowned author and lecturer on spirituality, healing and hospitality. In 1975 he wrote about all three of these subjects in his book, *Reaching Out*:

> In our world full of strangers, estranged from their own past, culture and country, from their neighbors, friends and family, from their deepest self and their God, we witness a painful search for a hospitable place where life can be lived without fear and where community can be found. Although many, we might even say most,

Camillus Volunteers help bring smiles to young and old alike.
(Photograph by Gina Fontana)

> strangers in this world become easily the victim of a fearful hostility, it is possible for men and women and obligatory for Christians to offer an open and hospitable place where strangers can cast off their strangeness and become our fellow human beings. The movement from hostility to hospitality is hard and full of difficulties. But still that is our voca-

tion: to convert the *hostis* into a *hospes*, the enemy into a guest, and to create the free and fearless space where brotherhood and sisterhood can be formed and fully experienced.[4]

What we are called upon to be or do as hosts.

Our Judeo-Christian heritage establishes the expectation that we be hospitable to strangers, suggesting that the stranger who comes may possess special attributes. Christians are especially invited to see Christ in the stranger. But what is the proper form for the hospitality we offer

Thanks to our benefactors, children always have a safe place at Camillus.
(Photograph by Gina Fontana)

such esteemed guests – what are we called on to do or provide as hosts?

For Henri Nouwen, hospitality entails more than the provision of food, comfort, warmth, friendship, and strength. For him, hospitality is a form of interaction in which the host creates a free and fearless space in which stranger-guests can be authentically themselves; a transforming place intended not to change guests, but to offer them space where change can take place; not an invitation to adopt the lifestyle of the host, but the gift of a chance for the guests to each find their own lifestyle.

The primary role of the host is to be open (Nouwen calls it *empty* in the way a glass is empty) for our guests; to listen to them; to attend to what they tell us in a way that makes these one-time strangers "familiar with the terrain they are travelling through and helps them to discover the way they want to go."[5] As for the guests, their role includes respect for the boundaries that the authentic host is expected to set. "We can enter into communication with the

A mom and son find a new home at Camillus House.
(Photograph by Gina Fontana)

other," Nouwen writes, "only when our own life choices, attitudes and viewpoints offer the boundaries that challenge strangers to become aware of their own position and to explore it critically." [6]

As a professional psychotherapist, I am struck by the similarities between Nouwen's description of the proper roles of the host and the preferred professional posture of the therapist healer. For me, the therapist provides an authentic, non-judgmental and transforming space (that contains appropriate boundaries) in which clients/patients can provide relevant information about their personal pasts, position themselves in relation to their present conditions and practice alternative approaches to the futures they anticipate or aspire to inhabit. Above all, the competent healer is a person who can listen perceptively, reflect accurately and counsel appropriately. Compare this to Henri Nouwen:

Healing is the humble but also very demanding task of creating and offering a friendly empty space where strangers can reflect on their pain and suffering without fear, and find the confidence that makes them look for new ways right in the center of their confusion[7]... The real host is the one who offers that space where we do not have to be afraid and where we can listen to our own inner voices and find our own personal way of becoming human. [8]

Dr. Paul
March 10, 2005

Céad Míle Fáilte: 100,000 Welcomes

Today is the day on which it is said that the whole world is Irish. For sure, this is true in America. Here, St. Patrick's feast is celebrated with great frivolity, friendship ("Kiss me, I'm *Irish!*"), feasting (on corned beef and cabbage), and insobriety, much of which would be alien to St. Patrick. "Google" the terms *hospitality* and either *St. Patrick* or *Irish*. You will plow through hundreds of links to St. Patrick's Day parades, lodging associated with these parades, and taverns at which parade goers can display their real or imagined Irishness, before you run across an article or sermon on the exemplar of hospitality in early Christian Ireland: St. Brigid.

Ancient Irish hospitality and concern for the poor.

This tradition has its roots in pre-Christian Ireland, where the general term for hospitality – '*oigidecht* – meant dealing with strangers. Secular law required freemen to provide hospitality to anyone who asked it of him; the type and quality of food and shelter one was obliged to offer varied depending on the class of his guest, and the status of the host. Failure to provide appropriate hospitality resulted in fines and ostracism. A guest came when he liked and left when he wished, all without the expectation of payment. Ancient Irish writers record that a man was reckoned wealthy not by what he had, but what he gave.

Irish attitudes toward the poor are captured in this old tune:

> Remember the poor when you look out on fields of your own, on your plump cows grazing.

> Remember the poor when you look into your barn, at the abundance of your harvest.

Remember the poor when the winds howl and the rain falls,
as you sit warm and dry in your house.

Remember the poor when you eat fine meat and drink fine ale
at your fine carved table.

The cows have grass to eat, the rabbits have burrows for shelter,
the birds have warm nests.

But the poor have no food except what you feed them, no shelter
except your house when you welcome them, no warmth except
your glowing fire.

A Christian form of this tradition was ultimately carried to the Continent by Irish missionary monks, and served as the basis for the hospitality shown pilgrims by monasteries throughout Christendom.

Brigid of Kildare.

St. Patrick returned to Ireland to convert the Celtic people there to Christianity around 432 A.D. Brigid was born in County Down twenty years later. The daughter of a king and a slave, in 470 A.D. she founded an abbey in Kildare, Ireland's first monastery for women. The Book of Lismore reports that the Lord granted every one of Brigid's wishes, but her steadfast request was "to satisfy the poor; to expel every hardship; to spare every miserable man." [9]

Alice Curtayne has written of Brigid's hospitality that:

> [T]he poor and the afflicted were her greatest friends, and for their sakes she disappointed everyone. Even the nuns objected to her methods... [W]hen some ec-

clesiastical dignitaries were due to visit her, the community took pains to prepare a feast worthy of the event. They scraped, planned, contrived, and at last, on the eve of the great day, all was in readiness. Then a host of beggars came swarming to the gates. Brigid spoke to them, and saw their plight at a compassionate glance. Hastening to the larder, and quite unmindful of her community's embarrassment, she distributed that carefully gathered feast among the mendicants, even down to the last crumb.[10]

St. Brigid of Kildare
(Source: Catholic Community Forum)

"It is in the name of Christ that I feed the poor," Brigid proclaimed, "for Christ is in the body of every poor man." Surely, she personified the words of this old Irish rune:

I saw a stranger yestereen;

I put food in the eating place, drink in the drinking place, music in the listening place,

And in the name of the Triune he blesses myself and my house, my cattle and my dear ones,

And the lark said in her song, often, often, often, goes the Christ in the stranger's guise,

Often, often, often, goes the Christ in the stranger's guise.

Dr. Paul
March 17, 2005

When our community opens itself up to strangers, our community benefits most.

We are at the end of our study of the virtue of hospitality. This Lent we have reviewed the traditions of hospitality of the ancient Greeks and Hebrews, and have learned from Saints Benedict and Brigid. Today we complete our investigation with the question: *Who gains most when a community opens itself to strangers?*

Strangers revitalize us and our communities.

Nouwen has captured the very real dilemma experienced by some persons in our community whose fear of strangers overwhelms their desire to provide hospitality:

> Although we may want to show sympathy for the poor, the lonely, the homeless and the rejected, our feelings toward a stranger knocking on our door and asking for food and shelter is ambivalent at the least... People who are unfamiliar, speak another language, have another color, wear a different kind of clothes and live a lifestyle different from ours, make us afraid...[11]

How might we overcome that ambivalence? One way is to recognize the important role strangers play in the vitality of our community and our individual lives. Jean Vanier answers this question with the following observation:

Welcome is one of the signs that a community is *alive*. To invite others to live with us is a sign that we aren't afraid, that we have a treasure of truth and of peace to share [emphasis added].[12]

Tracing his response to the same earliest Judeo-Christian roots that we have visited, Nouwen notes the benefit that comes to the generous host, shared simultaneously with the present guest:

[T]he biblical stories help us to realize not just that hospitality is an important virtue, but even more that in the context of hospitality guest and host can reveal their most precious gifts and bring *new life* to each other [emphasis added].[13]

Who gains most when a community opens itself to strangers? Paradoxically, when individuals offer hospitality to strangers, the greatest gain comes to the hosts themselves and to the hosts' communities. At Camillus House, we witness this every day as volunteers and staff greet our guests and clients and treat them to the hospitality of a nutritious meal, a night's rest, a refreshing shower and a change of clothes, a helpful intervention. For these hosts, Camillus House is a place to meet and serve others who are among the poor, the lonely, the homeless and the rejected, a place conveniently outfitted to engage in personal and community revitalization.

One of our volunteers has presented a proposition for all who want to revitalize our community through hospitality to strangers, but who remain timid in their presence or

(Photograph by Gina Fontana)

who reside in areas remote from the downtown streets where many persons who are poor, lonely, homeless and rejected spend their days and nights. His solution: "If not at your house, then at Camillus House." This brief statement captures the essence of the availability of Camillus House to the Miami community and to individuals who reside here and have the opportunity to revitalize themselves by serving the poor, the lonely, the homeless and the rejected of Miami, one guest at a time.

The ultimate act of hospitality.

As Christians around the world re-create the Last Supper in their Holy Thursday services tonight, they will re-enact Christ's washing the feet of his Apostles. This afternoon at Camillus House, the Brothers of the

Dr. Paul Ahr and his grandson Matthew (L) are shown here washing the feet of an individual who is homeless during the "Washing of the Feet" ceremony.

Good Shepherd and other Camillus managers and staff will wash the feet of 12 persons who are or have been homeless in Miami. Emulating the hospitality of Abraham and Lot and following the rule St. Benedict set for abbots, through this act we will witness to those who may be strangers in our world of Miami that we welcome them to our hospitable place where, in the words of Henri Nouwen, "life can be lived without fear and where community can be found."[14]

Dr. Paul
March 24, 2005

CHAPTER 5

Homeless but Not Hopeless

Reflections on being my brothers' and sisters' keeper

(Letters from the 2006 Lent Season)

We restart our Lenten journey calling to mind our own mortality.

Today is the first day of Lent, known in the Christian world as *Ash Wednesday*.

At precisely midnight last night, the period known as *Carnival*[15] came to an end, giving way to the penitential season of Lent. Catholics who attend Mass today will be marked on their foreheads with black ashes in the shape of a cross. The ashes are made by burning palm leaves retained from last year's Palm Sunday celebrations. These ashes are then mixed with olive oil. When applying the ashes, the priest or other person affixing them will say: "Remember, man, that you are dust, and unto dust you shall return."

For many persons in our Camillus family – Board members, Brothers and staff – our own mortality was made especially present over the last 12 months, as they said their final "goodbyes" to parents, other family members and other loved ones. As an orphan myself for more than a dozen years, my special thoughts go out to all whose last living parent has left this life. Many of these same feelings of sadness recurred for me when our Holy Father, Pope John Paul II died last April. Anyone who had the privilege of being in his presence, as I was in Rome and St. Louis, has been touched by the paternal love of this great man. And, at his funeral the

Pope John Paul II
(Source: Catholic Community Forum)

world touched back: four queens, five kings, 70 other heads of state were among the estimated 800,000 to 1,000,000 persons in Rome for this service.

Pope John Paul II is our guide.

This year, our Lenten journey will be guided by the readings and writings of Pope John Paul II. It is said that, set side-by-side, the authoritative collection of his teachings covers more than 30 linear feet of shelf space. That does not include his books of memoirs, theater and poetry. In particular, we will focus our reflections on the dignity of work, the transforming nature of suffering, the nature of charity and the essential nature of Divine Mercy. In addition, we will also visit the lives of some of his personal heroes – persons whom he proclaimed Blessed and Saint.[16]

When Pope John Paul II "returned to the house of the Father" on April 2, 2005, he served as the Roman Catholic Church's *Pontifex Maximus* (Latin for Supreme Bridgebuilder) or Pope longer than any previous Pontiff for whom there is historical data except Blessed Pius IX, who died in 1878. And as a bridgebuilder he built bridges spanning chasms that have separated Roman Catholics from other Christians and from Jews. He spanned the 20th and 21st Centuries with his pilgrimages (104 pastoral visits outside Italy and 146 within Italy) and his writings. This Lent we will affirm that his teachings serve as a bridge from his mind and heart directly to our door.

Venerable Matt Talbot and Saint Elizabeth Ann (Mother) Seton.

During the week that includes St. Patrick's Day, we will review the life of Venerable Matt Talbot (1856-1925), an Irishman of great charity and a role model for persons suffering from alcoholism. Beginning this year, the facility long known as the SRO has been renamed as Matt Talbot House. We will also reflect on the life of Saint Elizabeth Ann Seton (1774-1821), for whom our facility formerly called Airbase Families is now named.

Dr. Paul
March 1, 2006

On the nature and value of work.

Why we work.

According to Genesis 3:19, work is the penalty assessed against all the descendents of Adam and Eve for their disobeying God's will in the Garden of Eden. Because of their transgression, *all* men and women are destined to work for their sustenance. Until He began His public ministry, Christ worked as a carpenter and then as a teacher. St. Paul, who supported himself as a tentmaker, echoes Christ's teachings on the value of work, even to the point of advising the Thessalonians that "If any one will not work, let him not eat" (2 Thessalonians 3:10).

After the Germans invaded Poland in 1939, the young Karol Wojtyla, Jr. (later Pope John Paul, II) avoided deportation and imprisonment by working as a stone mason, an experience that had a great impact on him. In his 1981 encyclical *Laborem Exercens* (On Human Work) Pope John Paul II – this stone mason who became the supreme bridge builder (Pontifex Maximus) of the Roman Catholic Church – discussed the "new meanings of human work" in the modern world. This week we reflect on this encyclical especially as its themes apply to the work of Camillus House.

Work dignifies men and women.

For Pope John Paul II, work, "is an essential dimension of man's existence on earth," and is a means by which "*man*, created in the image of God, *shares by his work in the activity of the creator*" [emphasis in the original text].[17] The essential dignity of human work derives from the fact that, by working, men and women unique among all of God's creations, demonstrate how they are made in the image of the Creator. It is from this identification that we all first experience the dignity of our work: "For it shows what the dignity of work consists of: it teaches that man ought to imitate God, his Creator, in working, because man alone has the unique characteristic of likeness to God."

Laborem Exercens specifically addresses the positive – even redeeming – aspects of the call to work:

> Just as human activity proceeds from man, so it is ordered towards man. For when a man works, he not only alters things and society, he develops himself as well. He learns much, he cultivates his resources, and he goes outside of himself and beyond himself. Rightly understood, this kind of growth is of greater value than any external riches that can be garnered... Hence the norm of hu-

A young Hatian man named Jed had lost his job and eventually couldn't afford to pay rent for his apartment. The police found him sleeping in his car one night and recommended Camillus House. Afraid that he might be arrested if they found him again the next night, Jed came to Camillus House the next morning.

Camillus case managers helped Jed get a job as a security guard making a living wage and assisted him with the skills necessary to ensure he doesn't ever have to sleep in his car again. Also, within a few months and with the help of caring professionals at Camillus, Jed obtained his high school diploma. He was able to get back on his feet and regain a sense of dignity. Jed is now in his own apartment and has gone back to school to further improve his life.

(Photograph by Gina Fontana)

man activity is this: that in accord with the divine plan and will, it should harmonize with the genuine good of the human race, and allow people as individuals and as members of society to pursue their total vocation and fulfill it."

Further, work dignifies workers by providing them with the means to establish and maintain family life and to advance the process of education.

J.O.B. and jobs: prerequisites for breaking the cycle of homelessness.

As I was pulling together the Camillus House Strategic Plan in 2003 (approved in January 2004), the area of greatest identified need dealt with preparing Camillus House clients and other persons who are or may be homeless for good jobs. Camillus House's Job Opportunity Bureau (J.O.B.) is now well-launched as a resource for persons who need reliable work to pay for housing and other costs of living as well as supporting a family. Like all of Camillus' programs, J.O.B. has been designed to promote the dignity and self-sufficiency of persons who have been caught in the cycle of homelessness.

Our responsibilities as an employer.

For more than 125 employees, Camillus House helps provide the financial means to establish and properly maintain a family and provide security for its future. Over the next few weeks, senior Camillus House staff will be formulating our 2006-2007 budget, which will take effect in July. As we work on the budget, we will be especially concerned with ways to assure that all of our employees will be paid at a level that promotes a stable home life and the prospect of a better life for all in their household.

Dr. Paul
March 8, 2006

We surround ourselves with examples of ordinary people who lived extraordinary lives.

Earlier this year, the Brothers of the Good Shepherd responded favorably to our request to rename several of our facilities to honor persons revered by the Roman Catholic Church and by the Brothers themselves. In this week when we will celebrate the feast of St. Patrick, we call to mind Brother Mathias Barrett, the founder of the Congregation of the Little Brothers of the Good Shepherd, a native son of Waterford, Ireland and the Venerable Matt Talbot.

A role model for those persons suffering from an addiction.

Venerable Matt Talbot (1856-1925) was born in Dublin, Ireland. He was the second of 12 children born into a poor family; his father worked on the docks. Because his father had a hard time supporting his family, Matt left school after only a few years of formal education. Matt worked as a messenger for some liquor merchants; and began drinking excessively at the age of 15. For the next 15 years he was an active alcoholic. At age 30 he embraced sobriety and remained sober for the rest of his life.

Venerable Matt Talbot
(Source: Catholic Community Forum)

Some credit Matt Talbot with developing a step-like recovery program that was a precursor of the contemporary 12-step program. According to his biographers, remaining sober was an especially difficult challenge during the first seven years of Matt's commitment to sobriety. Avoiding his former drinking places was hard. He turned to prayer as a support in his program of sobriety.

For most of his adult life, Matt worked as a builder's laborer. Although he was in no way a man of even moderate financial means, Matt Talbot conscientiously repaid debts he generated during the years that he was an active alcoholic, and gave generously to charitable causes. Once his health failed in 1923, Matt quit work, and he died on his way to Mass on June 7, 1925. Fifty years later, Pope Paul VI declared him Venerable. The building once known as SRO is now named Matt Talbot House.

Wife, widow, single mother, Saint.

Elizabeth Bayley Seton (1774-1821) was the first native-born American to be canonized by the Catholic Church. Born two years before the American Revolution, Elizabeth grew up in the "cream" of New York's Protestant society. Her father was the first professor of anatomy at Columbia College.

In 1794, Elizabeth married the wealthy young William Seton, with whom she was deeply in love. The first years of their marriage were happy and prosperous. Within four years, Will's father died, leaving the young couple in charge of Will's seven half brothers and sisters, as well as the family's importing business. Now events began to move fast and with devastating effect. Both Will's business and his health failed. He was finally forced to file a petition of bankruptcy. In a final attempt to save Will's health, the Setons sailed for Italy, where Will had business associates. In December 1803,

Will died of tuberculosis while in Italy. Elizabeth and Will were married for one month less than ten years, and their union produced five children.

Saint Elizabeth Ann (Mother) Seton
(photograph by Dr. Peter G. Ahr)

Elizabeth's deep concern for the spiritual welfare of her family and friends eventually led her into the Catholic Church. Her conversion to Catholicism was at a dear price, for Elizabeth was abandoned by most of her Protestant relatives. Needing to support her young family, Elizabeth responded to the invitation of the president of St. Mary's College in Baltimore, Maryland, to found a school in that city. She and two other young women began plans for a religious order of women. They established the first free Catholic school in America. When the young religious community adopted their rule, they made provisions for Elizabeth to continue raising her children. On March 25, 1809, Elizabeth Seton pronounced her vows of poverty, chastity, and obedience. From that time she was called Mother Seton. Mother Seton died in 1821 at the age of 46, only sixteen years after becoming a Catholic. She was canonized on September 14, 1975. The Roman Catholic Church celebrates her feast day on January 4th of each year. The facility formerly named Airbase Families is now known as Mother Seton Village.

Dr. Paul
March 15, 2006

We are profoundly consistent in our promotion of human dignity for all.

Those familiar with the Charisms of the Brothers of the Good Shepherd that orient Camillus House's work in the world know that they are five: hospitality (which we addressed at length last Lent), availability, flexibility, adaptability and respect for human dignity. This last charism, also put in practice as the ongoing promotion of human dignity, was a favorite topic for reflection and action by Pope John Paul II.

Evangelium Vitae: The Gospel of Life.

Eleven years ago this week, Pope John Paul II issued the encyclical *Evangelium Vitae*: (The Gospel of Life). In it, he addressed the essential basis for ascribing an inherent dignity in all men and women; all of us merit dignity because we have been formed in the image and likeness of the Creator:

> Man's life comes from God; it is his gift, his image and imprint, a sharing in his breath of life. God therefore is the sole Lord of this life: man cannot do with it as he wills. God himself makes this clear to Noah after the Flood: "For your own lifeblood, too, I will demand an accounting... and from man in regard to his fellow man I will demand an accounting for human life" (Genesis 9:5). The biblical text is concerned to emphasize how the sacredness of life has its foundation in God and in his creative activity: "For God made man in his own image" (Genesis 9:6)[18].

And he reminded us that the "all" who are formed in the Creator's likeness especially includes brothers and sisters who are frail, disabled, dependent because of youth or old age, homeless and otherwise without the means to provide for themselves. Reminding us that we are our brothers' and sisters' keepers, he applauds those among us who provide caring charity to others. He especially singles out individuals who:

> over and above their everyday service to life, are willing to accept abandoned children, boys and girls and teenagers in difficulty, handicapped persons, elderly men and women who have been left alone... Increasingly, there are appearing in many places groups of volunteers prepared to offer hospitality to persons without a family, who find themselves in conditions of particular distress or who need a supportive environment to help them to overcome destructive habits and discover anew the meaning of life.

The necessity for faith and good works.

Further, Pope John Paul II reiterated that our support and promotion of human life and dignity "must be accomplished through the service of charity,

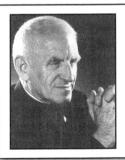

Brother Mathias Barrett, BGS Founder of Camillus House.

From the beginning, Brother Mathias insisted on one thing: Camillus House would serve all who needed help, without regard to race, creed, color, or religion.
At Camillus, that ideal that all men and women are equal and worthy in God's eyes, became a reality.

(Source: Camillus House)

which finds expression in personal witness, various forms of volunteer work, social activity and political commitment." He continued with words that are especially resonant in the good works of the Brothers of the Good Shepherd performed through the Camillus House staff, volunteers and benefactors:

> As the Letter of James admonishes us: "What does it profit, my brethren, if a man says he has faith but has not works? Can his faith save him? If a brother or sister is ill-clad and in lack of daily food, and one of you says to them, "Go in peace, be warmed and filled," without giving them the things needed for the body, what does it profit? So faith by itself, if it has no works, is dead" (James 2:14-17).

> In our service of charity, we must be inspired and distinguished by a specific attitude: we must care for the other as a person for whom God has made us responsible... we are called to become neighbors to everyone (cf. Luke 10:29-37), and to show special favor to those who are poorest, most alone and most in need. In helping the hungry, the thirsty, the foreigner, the naked, the sick, the imprisoned – as well as the child in the womb and the old person who is suffering or near death – we have the opportunity to serve Jesus. He himself said: "As you did it to one of the least of these my brethren, you did it to me" (Matthew 25:40). Hence, we cannot but feel called to account and judged by the ever relevant words of Saint John Chrysostom: "Do you wish to honor the body of Christ? Do not neglect it when you find it naked. Do not do it homage here in the church with silk fabrics only to neglect it outside where it suffers cold and nakedness."

Dr. Paul
March 22, 2006

Human suffering affords us the privilege to be as available as the Good Samaritan.

Why does a compassionate God permit suffering to exist in the world? In fact, why would a compassionate Father allow his only Son to suffer a cruel and humiliating death, especially after His Son prayed fervently to be spared His suffering? In his 1984 encyclical *Salvifici Doloris* (On the Christian Meaning of Human Suffering), Pope John Paul II answers these questions in part in the following way:

> In the... program of the *Kingdom of God*, suffering is present in the world in order to release love, in order to give birth to works of love towards neighbor, in order to transform the whole of human civilization into a "civilization of love"... [W]e could say that suffering, which is present under so many different forms in our human world, is also present in order *to unleash love in the human person*, that unselfish gift of one's "I" on behalf of other people, especially those who suffer.[19]

Who are our neighbors, and what is our obligation to them?

According to the Holy Father, Christ chose the parable of the Good Samaritan, to address the question, "Who is my neighbor?" Christ showed that the Samaritan was the "real neighbor" of the victimized stranger, precisely because this Samaritan was the one who was compassionate to his neighbor, in fulfillment of the great commandment to *love one's neighbor*. One of the great paradoxes of compassionate encounters is that each is

A Camillus House volunteer feeding a needy child.
(Photograph by Elise Linder)

an *interaction of two* neighbors, each assisting the other. The Samaritan helps the wounded man to recover his health and dignity, while the wounded man helps the Samaritan get in touch with and express his compassion – love – for another; that is, to "unleash... the unselfish gift of one's 'I' or self." In the deepest of our traditions, the person (especially a stranger) toward whom we show compassion is a representative of Christ, who was Himself a victim.

We visited this theme of reciprocity last year (see page 99) when we learned from St. Benedict that hospitality is reciprocal: the host and guest represent Christ to each other. Benedictine hospitality is based on the principle that for me to be a whole person, I have to let others in. Thus the host and guest require each other; in fact, the Indo-European root of both words host and guest are the same: *ghosti.*

We are each compelled to be a Good Samaritan.

This Lent we examine the reciprocal nature of *availability.* Sufferers are present among us; we see them every day. For Pope John Paul II, we have no choice but to be available to them:

> We are not allowed to "pass by on the other side" indifferently; we must "stop" beside him. *Everyone who stops beside the suffering*

of another person, whatever form it may take, is a Good Samaritan. This stopping does not mean curiosity but *availability* [emphasis added]. It is like the opening of a certain interior disposition of the heart, which also has an emotional expression of its own. The name "Good Samaritan" fits every *individual who is sensitive to the sufferings of others*, who "is moved" by the misfortune of another.

This attitude of availability is one of the charisms of the Brothers of the Good Shepherd as set forth by their founder.

Finally, the Pope reminded us to be aware of the urgency of compassion, recalling Christ's description of how those who are compassionate toward sufferers and those who are not will be treated at the time of the Final Judgment (cf. Matthew 25:34-46):

"Come, O blessed of my Father, inherit the kingdom prepared for you from the foundation of the world; for I was hungry and you fed me food, I was thirsty and you gave me drink, I was a stranger and you welcomed me, I was in prison and you came to me." To the just, who ask when they did all this to Him, the Son of Man will respond: "Truly, I say to you, *as you did it to one of the least of these my brethren*, you did it to Me." The opposite sentence will be imposed on those who have behaved differently: "As you did it not to one of the least of these, you did it not to Me."

Dr. Paul
March 29, 2006

Our Saints are our guides.

For the past two weeks, within the context of the encyclicals of Pope John Paul II, we have had the opportunity to address two of the five charisms of the Congregation of the Little Brothers of the Good Shepherd: respect for human dignity and availability. During his Papacy, John Paul II canonized 482 persons as Saints. Among them were several persons who, like the Pope, were sons and daughters of Poland. Two Polish Saints canonized by Pope John Paul II help us "put a face on" the charisms of hospitality, availability and respect for human dignity.

Saint Albert Chmielowski.

Adam Chmielowski was born into a wealthy Polish aristocratic family in 1845. As a young man he was drawn to politics and art. He was imprisoned for his role in failed uprisings against the Russian occupation. Later he dis-

Saint Albert Chmielowski
(Source: Catholic Community Forum)

tinguished himself as an artist, having studied painting in Warsaw, Munich and Paris. These joint passions – politics and art – brought him in contact with the needs of those much less fortunate than himself. Filled with compassion, Adam felt a calling from God to turn to a life of service.

Adam abandoned his painting and began working with the poorest people in the city of Krakow. At first Adam became a member of the Third Order of St. Francis, and in 1887 he founded the *Brothers of the Third Order of Saint Francis, Servants of the Poor*, known as the *Albertines* (in honor of the name he took when entering religious life – Brother Albert) or the *Gray Brothers* (after their rough gray habits). In 1891 he founded the women's congregation of the Order. St. Albert's vocation was heavily influenced by the example of another Polish friar: St. Rafael Kalinowski. Dependent solely on alms, the Albertines organized food and shelter for the poor and homeless, a mission that continues to the present day.

As a young priest, Pope John Paul II wrote a play dealing with the life of Brother Albert entitled *Our God's Brother*. St. Albert died on Christmas Day in 1916, and was canonized on November 12, 1989.

Saint Maximilian Kolbe.

The future Saint Maximilian was born as Raymond Kolbe in 1894, the second of three sons born to a poor but pious Catholic family in Russian occupied Poland. He began his preparation for priestly life in 1907, taking his first vows in the *Conventual Franciscan Order* at age 16, adopting the name Maximilian. He was ordained a priest in 1918, returning to Poland the next year, to teach history in the Krakow seminary. Despite battling tuberculosis for most of his adult years, Father Maximilian published a magazine to fight religious apathy, founded three monasteries (in Poland, Japan and India) and a minor seminary, started a newspaper, and was a missionary to Japan, all before he was 40 years old.

Following the Nazi invasion of Poland he was interred briefly, and returned to the monastery he founded, where they provided food and shelter for 3,000 Polish refugees, two-thirds of whom were Jewish. There he continued pub-

Saint Maximilian Kolbe in his 30's, just before leaving for Japan.
(Source: Catholic Community Forum)

lishing, including materials considered anti-Nazi. For these activities, Maximilian was imprisoned first in Pawiak prison, Warsaw, Poland and later in Auschwitz, where he was branded as prisoner 16670. He was assigned to a special work group staffed by priests and supervised by especially vicious and abusive guards. His manner brought him the worst jobs and more beatings than anyone else. At one point he was beaten, whipped and left for dead.

In July 1941 there was an escape from the concentration camp. Camp protocol required that ten men be slaughtered in retribution for each escaped prisoner. Francis Gajowniczek, a married man with young children was chosen to die for the escape. Maximilian volunteered to take his place. He was thrown down the stairs to the basement of his cell block, and left to die of thirst and starvation with nine other prisoners. When the stairwell was needed two weeks later for more victims, only Maximilian was alive and conscious. He was put to death with a lethal injection of carbolic acid. Ironically, this frail Polish priest once wrote that "The most deadly poison of our times is indifference." He was canonized in the presence of Francis Gajowniczek by Pope John Paul II on October 10, 1982. He is the Patron Saint of persons who are chemically addicted.

Dr. Paul
April 5, 2006

Blessed are the merciful,
for they shall obtain mercy.

Pope John Paul II died on the evening of April 2, 2005, shortly after celebrating the liturgy for the vigil of Divine Mercy Sunday. In 1980, the Pope established this Feast as he elevated to Sainthood Sister Maria Faustina, a simple Polish nun to whom Jesus had appeared. He directed her to have a picture painted (a copy of which hangs in our own Chapel of Divine Mercy), and instructed her as follows:

> Summon all those to confidence in the incomprehensible depth of my mercy for I desire to save all... I do not exclude anyone... Tell ailing mankind to draw close to my merciful heart and I will fill them with peace... Let not even the weak and very sinful fear to approach me, even if their sins be as numerous as all the sand of the earth all will be forgiven in the fathomless pit of my mercy.[20]

The greatest inheritance: richness in mercy.

In his 1980 encyclical *Dives in Misericordia*: (Rich in Mercy), Pope John Paul II illuminated the concept of Divine Mercy through the Parable of the Prodigal Son. This is a parable that I frankly did not understand when I was growing up with my four brothers. Once I had sons of my own it became clearer; the Pope made it clearer still.

Perhaps the simplest way to understand Divine Mercy is to explain it as a higher form of justice or fairness, elevated by love. Mercy is the outcome of a relationship between two people: one who has harmed, failed or otherwise transgressed against the other, and the other from whom the first asks forgiveness based on a willingness to reform his or her life. In the parable, the son squandered his inheritance and his dignity, grievously paining his father. Ultimately, the son concluded that he relinquished all standing with his father, expecting to be treated on his return only as a common laborer. What the son did not calculate, however, was that when his father handed over his financial inheritance, he *could not* give away his love for his son. This love burst forth when the father first saw his returning son: "But while he was still a long way off, his father saw him and was filled with compassion for him; he ran to his son, threw his arms around him and kissed him" (Luke 15:20). Throughout, the father was faithful to himself – he remained a loving father despite the actions of his son. John Paul II explained this relationship as follows:

> The father's fidelity to himself is totally concentrated upon the humanity of the lost son, upon his dignity... one can therefore say that the love for the son is the love that springs from the very essence of fatherhood, in a way it obliges the father to be concerned about his son's dignity. This concern is the measure of his love... [which] is able to reach down to every prodigal son, to every human misery, and above all to every form of moral misery, to sin. When this happens, the person who is the object of mercy does not feel humiliated, but rather found again and "restored to value."

When Marta's husband lost his construction job, the family was unable to pay rent. Marta and her husband, Herberto, their 10-year-old daughter, Elizabeth (who suffers from cerebral palsy), their two teenage sons and the children's grandmother faced the very real possibility of homelessness. Just when things looked bleakest, someone told them about Camillus House. Now the family who fled Cuba to Miami has food, their own apartment and much more. For the first time in her life, Elizabeth is looking at the possibility of attending school. The entire family is learning the financial skills necessary so this will never happen to them again. "Camillus House is a blessing," Marta says.

(Photograph by Gina Fontana)

The father first and foremost expresses to him his joy that he has been "found again" and that he has "returned to life." This joy indicates a good that has remained intact: even if he is a prodigal, a son does not cease to be truly his father's son; it also indicates a good that has been found again, which in the case of the prodigal son was his return to the truth about himself.

The parable of the prodigal son expresses in a simple but profound way the reality of conversion. Conversion is the most concrete expression of the working of love and of the presence of mercy in the human world. The true and proper meaning of mercy does not consist only in looking, however penetratingly and compassionately, at moral, physical or material evil: mercy is manifested in its true and proper aspect when it restores to value, promotes and draws good from all the forms of evil existing in the world and in man.

When God meets His sons and daughters at Camillus House, we serve as their hosts.

Camillus House is a plain on which our merciful God searches for and embraces His sons and daughters who seek to restore in their lives the good – the inherent dignity – that is their birthright. We celebrate our vocations as hosts and helpers, because when we reach out to these brothers and sisters as they seek to turn around or convert their lives, we comfort them as with the outstretched arms of Divine Mercy. Rest in peace, Holy Father, your devotion is at the center of our work here, both in our Chapel of Divine Mercy, and in the efforts of our Brothers, volunteers and staff.

Dr. Paul
April 12, 2006

CHAPTER 6

The Journey Home

Rest stops on the road to our Father's house

(Letters from the 2007 Lent Season)

We prepare for the blessings of Easter in the season of Lent.

As I drove to my office to write this piece, I was listening to a radio interview conducted by travel writer Rick Steves. He was speaking with a woman who owns a hat shop in the French Quarter of New Orleans, and they were discussing the post-Katrina revival of that city's Mardi Gras celebrations.

The hat lady says that she is having a hard time making ends meet since tourism has been slow to rebound. She hopes for a crowd that is at least half of what they had in 2004, and for two-thirds of the 2004 level in 2008. She tells Steves that she is optimistic and prepared for a better Mardi Gras than she expects, but she is patient and willing to stick it out. When asked by Steves whether she is put off by the tours of the still-devastated neighborhoods in New Orleans, she says that at first she was, but now she's not. Her rationale is that people from outside New Orleans will better understand the terrible impact Hurricane Katrina had on their city, and thereby better appreciate the improvements that have been made to date. This discussion sounded an awful lot like Lent, which begins on Ash Wednesday, February 21. Only by confronting and correcting our failings can we can we properly prepare for and appreciate the great blessings of Easter.

Although this piece will be dated on Ash Wednesday, the radio story about New Orleans compelled me to write it today, Sunday, February 18, 2007. One reason for writing it early is that Peter England and I will be in Tallahassee on Tuesday and Wednesday, promoting State financial support for our new buildings, and for the programs that we will operate there in three years or so. More importantly to me, my father died on this date in 1979, and that memory and the radio interview about New Orleans brought to my mind an unpleasant experience I had in that great city.

My father left me a few things, the most valuable of which was his professional grade 35mm camera. I brought it along on a trip to New Orleans shortly thereafter, and took it out with me one evening to photograph the French Quarter at night. Foolishly, I wandered into a part of town not frequented by tourists – at least not by tourists traveling solo. Three men passed me on the street, turned and knocked off my glasses as they pushed

Sea of Galilee from the
Mount of the Beatitudes
(Photograph by Dr. Paul R. Ahr)

me to the ground. I readily (but not happily) gave up my watch and cash, but held tightly to my dad's camera, which I had "hidden" under my trench coat. They left richer and me wiser.

I love New Orleans, and have been back often, several times during the Mardi Gras season. When I am there at that time of year, I cannot help but reflect on how my "incident" on a dark street was also like Lent: foolishness had put me at risk, and I paid (did penance) for that foolishness. Of the things I had with me that night, most were expendable, but one, my father's gift to me, was worth a fight. Happily it didn't come to that, and for that I continue to feel blessed. Lent is a good time for me to reflect on what my father, now in Heaven, and Our Father who art in Heaven have given me as my inheritance, and whether I have protected those gifts; whether I would put up a fight to protect them.

Over the 40 days and 40 nights of Lent, I will be writing down my thoughts about what it means to be "blessed," using as my guide the eight Beatitudes detailed in Matthew 5. When I last wrote about Lent (see pages 131-133), I focused on one of the Beatitudes: Blessed are the merciful, for they shall obtain mercy. Over the next six weeks, I will reflect on the remaining seven.

In 1985, I took my father's camera with me to the Holy Land, and there took a photograph of the Sea of Galilee from the top of the Mount of Beatitudes, once known as Mt. Eremos. A copy of my photo of this serene and special place in displayed in the third floor lobby of the Camillus Health Concern building. I invite you to join me on that mountain as we pass through this Lenten season.

Dr. Paul
February 21, 2007

Blessed are the poor in spirit: for theirs is the Kingdom of Heaven. Blessed are the meek: for they will inherit the land.

The Beatitudes (Matthew 5:3-10) form only the first set of lessons given by Jesus on the top of Mt. Eremos. Later in Chapter 5, Jesus refers to His followers as "the salt of the earth," and exhorts us to love our enemies. Before departing the mountain top (Chapters 6 & 7), Jesus teaches us the *Our Father*, and advises us:

> Do not store up for yourselves treasures on earth, where moth and decay destroy, and thieves break in and steal. But store up treasures in heaven, where neither moth nor decay destroys, nor thieves break in and steal. For where your treasure is, there also will your heart be (Matthew 6:19-21).

Who are the poor in spirit?

At Camillus House, we are privileged to work with persons of very limited financial means; people who are considered and classified as "poor." Are they entitled to the kingdom because they are poor? Not necessarily. They are not entitled to it just because they are poor, because poverty itself is not blessed. However once they, or we, or anyone realizes that we cannot achieve salvation on our own – once we acknowledge that we have sinned and rely on God's grace for salvation – then we can be considered and called persons who are poor in spirit, and can aspire to the kingdom of

God. It is then that we become like the Prodigal Son who, by admitting his unworthiness, earned the mercy of his father (as we discussed – see page 131), and in the context of this Beatitude, re-established his worthiness to receive an inheritance from his father.

I believe that the greatest strengths of Camillus House are our openness: (a) to the wisdom of God to direct our actions on behalf of our guests and clients; (b) to the goodness of God who amply provides for the needs of our guests and clients; and (c) to the ready availability to God's divine mercy through both the daily opportunity to practice the charisms of the Brothers of the Good Shepherd and our easy access to the spiritual guidance of the Brothers, Sisters, Priests and other ministers who exemplify here how to live a life of a person who is poor in spirit.

Homeless and alone, 71-year-old James (Left with Brother Bill) was taken to the hospital with a chronic obstructive pulmonary disorder that had been troubling him for decades. With no medical insurance, no Social Security card, no savings and no family ties, James had nowhere to go. He was released to a medical bed at Camillus House, where he was able to convalesce. The people at Camillus House also guided him through reclaiming his identity and accessing all the government benefits to which he was entitled. James, who was a boxer in his youth, has a new lease on life and is ready to fight the next round.

(Photograph by Gina Fontana)

Who are the meek?

Many years ago, my father lovingly counseled me that, to be truly success-ful, I would have to master the virtues of patience and humility. He was right, and I consider myself a "work in progress" on both counts. As I work (sometimes impatiently) on the virtue of humility, I wrestle with the real-ization that for me to succeed I must subordinate my will, my knowledge, my experience, even my impatience to a greater good. Much of what I have to do is wrapped up in this Beatitude.

Is the meek person a weak person? Actually, the opposite is true. The Greek word for "meek" used in the original text refers to a domesticated, but pow-erful and productive animal, like a horse or ox. The meaning here is that the meek person is the person who is developed, determined, decisive, and disci-plined: the person who submits not to his own will or the will of the world, but to the will of God. Putting their faith in God, persons who are meek can also afford to be patient, since they have chosen the path to success.

Every day at Camillus House we have the opportunity to be with guests and clients who, by submitting to the will of God by "letting go and letting God," demonstrate the strength that comes with meekness. Pat Cawley and Kathy Garcia[21] both point out that those clients who turn over their lives to God have faster, greater and longer rates of addiction recovery than those who are unable or unwilling to do so. Pat and Kathy also report that the presence of the Brothers and Sisters, and especially the availability of *Centering Prayer*, greatly facilitate our clients' decisions to let God – rather than their addictions – control their lives.

Dr. Paul
February 28, 2007

Blessed are those who mourn, for they shall be comforted.

I have been close to grieving persons since childhood. My grandfather and father built a prosperous funeral business in Essex County, NJ, where, for a while during my college years, I served as an apprentice funeral director. Many times my brothers and I went out on night calls to pick up the bodily remains of a deceased person, often in their own homes where they died surrounded by their loved ones. At those times, like our father and grandfather before us, we were present with those left behind as their love and fear were transformed to grief and mourning.

"No one should have to die alone, unmourned and unremembered."

I learned early about the consoling effects of faith, family and friendship, each offering comfort in their own ways. Our Catholic Christian funeral rituals can be powerfully cathartic, sometimes evoking a residual reaction in participants who are not the primary mourners at a funeral Mass. In many cases grief allows all, even persons who are not particularly religious, to recognize God as the Father of compassion described in the second letter of Paul to the Corinthians; the same God acknowledged by Job, who called out in his grief: "My ears had heard of you but now my eyes have seen you" (Job 42:5).

In his book, *Waking Up in America*, our own Dr. Joe Greer challenges us in this way: "No one should have to die alone, unmourned and unremembered." [22] It remains an important act of charity that Camillus House and the Brothers of the Good Shepherd hold spiritually-oriented memorial services for persons who we have served who have died, but who don't have a family or other supports, other than Camillus House, to be mourned.

Recently, I had dinner with Irene Arditi, whose husband Maurice has been an advisor to and supporter of Camillus House. Over the past year or so, Irene has buried both of her parents in France. She told me of the healing effects of repeating activities and traditions she had enjoyed with her parents, and of the comforting effect of viewing photographs of them. Irene and I had come from an event that included a poster-size copy of the cover for the auto-biography of our friend Peggy Tredler. The cover is comprised of a collage of photos of family members and friends, many now deceased. I watched with wonder as Peggy would gently touch the photos of those whom death has taken from her. Although now almost four years later, in her auto-biography Peggy and her daughter Edie recall in vivid detail the circumstances surrounding Mr. Tredler's death, as if it happened only yesterday.

Michelangelo's Pieta, St. Peter's Basilica, the Vatican
(Photograph by Stanislav Traykov
Source: Wiki Media Commons)

No one should die unremembered, Joe Greer teaches us, and following his advice, and the experiences of Irene and Peggy, we will begin to publicly remember persons who we have served with a memorial that displays their names and photos. This memorial will be both a tribute to those who have passed on, and a promise to our current and future clients that they will not be unremembered.

Mourning is the price we pay for loving well.

"When you are sorrowful look again in your heart," Kahil Gibran tells us, "and you shall see that in truth you are weeping for that which has been your delight." This lesson was made evident to Peter England and me recently when we visited the Tallahassee office of State Senator Frederica Wilson, a great friend to Camillus House. She had just returned to the Capitol from planning and attending the funeral of her brother, Thirlee Smith, Jr., the first African American reporter for the Miami *Herald*. At that moment, she was only beginning the work described so eloquently by Margery Allingham: "Mourning is not forgetting... It is an undoing. Every minute tie has to be untied and something permanent and valuable recovered and assimilated from the dust." Because of the special relationship between Camillus House and Senator Wilson, we have asked to remember her brother by incorporating his photo amidst our photographic history of Black Miami at our Brownsville Christian Housing Center, allowing us to help her recover and preserve in perpetuity there this most valuable relationship between brother and sister.

How might we lighten the burden of our "grief work?" One way is to be a delight to "that which has been your delight." Harriet Beecher Stowe rightly observes that "The bitterest tears shed over graves are for words left unsaid and deeds left undone." Do not leave words unsaid or deeds undone, so that when you grieve, you will grieve because you have lost one who you truly loved rather than because you did not love him/her when he/she was in your midst.

Dr. Paul
March 7, 2007

Happy Birthday, Brother Mathias.

Have you ever been to a birthday party where the gifts are for the guests? That is the way I feel each year on March 15th. This day is the birthday of Brother Mathias Barrett, BGS, the founder of the Congregation of the Little Brothers of the Good Shepherd and of Camillus House. And for more than 46 years, the people of Miami have been the recipient of Brother Mathias' generosity and love of the poor.

Brother Mathias was born Maurice Patrick Barrett on March 15, 1900 in Waterford, a city on the southern coast of Ireland, internationally known for its Waterford crystal. Until age 16, he lived with his parents, Tom and Margaret, his brother John and sister Mary. At age 14, Maurice first felt a calling to religious life and made inquiries to the Holy Cross Brothers in Notre Dame, Indiana, and the Hospitaller Order of St. John of God in England, who invited him to visit their house in Dublin. On March 17, 1916 Maurice entered this Order and, as Brother Mathias, served with distinction in the Hospitaller's ministries in Europe, Canada and the United States.

In September 1950, Brother Mathias arrived in New Mexico to assist in the care of elderly priests. Soon Archbishop Edwin V. Byrne of Santa Fe encouraged him to start his own order of Brothers to work with "men on the road" in Albuquerque. On January 19, 1951 Brother Mathias founded the Congregation of the Little Brothers of the Good Shepherd (BGS), a Roman Catholic pontifical institute of religious Brothers, whose members profess vows of chastity, poverty and obedience. As is recorded on our website (www. camillus.org), Brother Mathias' ministry in Miami began in 1960:

Brother Mathias went to Miami in the late 1950s at the request of Miami's first Bishop, Coleman Carroll, who was concerned about the large influx of Cuban refugees into the diocese who came to the city with no food and no place to stay. In 1960 Brother Mathias founded Camillus House, serving the first meal of donated cornflakes with donated milk to an elderly man. Several weeks later he moved Camillus House to 726 N.E. First Ave. and the charity has since fed, clothed, housed, and provided medical treatment to hundreds of thousands of needy people.

In the early 1970s, Brother Mathias sought to expand the services at Camillus House to include a small residential program. He wrote to then-Archbishop Carroll of his desire to establish at Camillus House a program where men "could be sheltered and cared for during the day, as well as at night." When he died in retirement in 1990, his dream for Miami was only one of the many victories for poor and homeless persons won by this legendary figure who had achieved worldwide fame as "A living example of the Beatitudes." [23]

By 2007, Brother Mathias' desire for a program of residential as well as day services, first envisaged for a handful of homeless men, has grown into a comprehensive system of care including shelter, job training, mental health, physical health and substance abuse treatment and housing. Annually, Camillus House and Camillus Health Concern have a combined budget of nearly $15,000,000 and serve more than 10,000 men, women and children. Each year, Camillus provides more than 400,000 free meals, and 300,000 nights of lodging.

But Brother Mathias' greatest gifts to us are the charisms of the Congregation of the Brothers of the Good Shepherd that guide our work: hospitality, availability, flexibility, adaptability and respect for human dignity. As we celebrate the 107th anniversary of the birth of Brother Mathias Barrett, BGS, I invite you to join me in this prayer:

Dear God: You sent us your humble servant Brother Mathias Barrett to tend to the needs of persons who are poor and sick and homeless in Miami. Brother Mathias so loved the people of Miami that he established here Camillus House, a place of refuge and recovery to give witness to Your loving, healing and consoling power. The seed planted by Brother Mathias has grown into a tree of great height and reach, covering all who seek Your comfort and protection. Please send us the Holy Spirit to illuminate our minds and stimulate our hearts as we tend the tree and nurture the persons who seek the relief that precedes growth and the growth that precedes mastery under its ever expanding cover. Amen.

Happy Birthday, Brother Mathias. Thank you for your gifts to Miami: Camillus House and the Brothers of the Good Shepherd.

Dr. Paul
March 15, 2007

Blessed are they that hunger and thirst after justice: for they shall have their fill. Blessed are they that suffer persecution for justice's sake, for theirs is the Kingdom of Heaven.

I have joined together here the fourth and eighth Beatitudes, both of which focus on an important issue: the pursuit of justice. As a psychologist, I am struck that the fourth Beatitude references physical drives that are at the base of Maslow's hierarchy of needs – thirst and hunger – to underscore the urgency and importance with which we should pursue the cause of justice. Those who suffer persecution in the pursuit of justice are promised the reward of the Kingdom of Heaven.

Catholic social teaching.

The Church's social teaching is comprehensive and instructive concerning the creation and maintenance of a just society. As caregivers to many persons whose cause demands social justice, we are emboldened by the guidance of our American Bishops in this regard. The United States Conference of Catholic Bishops (Publication No. 5-315) has identified seven (7) key themes that they consider to be "at the heart of our Catholic social tradition," and are repeated here. They are:

1. *Life and Dignity of the Human Person:* The Catholic Church proclaims that human life is sacred and that the dignity of the human person is the foundation of a moral vision for society. This belief is the foundation of all the principles of our social teaching…We believe that every person

is precious, that people are more important than things, and that the measure of every institution is whether it threatens or enhances the life and dignity of the human person.

2. *Call to Family, Community, and Participation:* The person is both sacred and social. How we organize our society in economics and politics, in law and policy directly affects human dignity and the capacity of individuals to grow in community. Marriage and the family are the central social institutions that must be supported and strengthened, not undermined. We believe people have a right and a duty to participate in society, seeking together the common good and well-being of all, especially the poor and vulnerable.

L-R sitting: Giovan and Brother Charles Searson; L-R standing: Brother Bill Osmanski and Brother Majella Marchand.

Twenty-one-year-old Giovan was attacked by four men. They robbed him of everything he had and beat him so badly he lost his four front teeth and almost his life. He woke up at Jackson Memorial Hospital where he was treated.

He was discharged with no money and nowhere to go. Then he remembered someone at the hospital had told him about Camillus House. There he found shelter, medical care and people who cared about him. Thanks to our benefactors, Camillus House was able to give Giovan a brand-new start, not to mention a brand-new smile.

(Photograph by Gina Fontana)

3. *Rights and Responsibilities:* The Catholic tradition teaches that human dignity can be protected and a healthy community can be achieved only if human rights are protected and responsibilities are met. Corresponding to these rights are duties and responsibilities – to one another, to our families, and to the larger society.

4. *Option for the Poor and Vulnerable:* A basic moral test is how our most vulnerable members are faring. In a society marred by deepening divisions between rich and poor, our tradition recalls the story of the Last Judgment (Matthew 25:31-46) and instructs us to put the needs of the poor and vulnerable first.

5. *The Dignity of Work and the Rights of Workers:* Work is more than a way to make a living; it is a form of continuing participation in God's creation. If the dignity of work is to be protected, then the basic rights of workers must be respected – the right to productive work, to decent and fair wages, to the organization and joining of unions, to private property, and to economic initiative.

6. *Solidarity:* We are our brothers' and sisters' keepers, wherever they may be. Loving our neighbor has global dimensions in a shrinking world. At the core of the virtue of solidarity is the pursuit of justice and peace. As Pope Paul VI taught, "If you want peace, work for justice."

7. *Care for God's Creation:* We show our respect for the Creator by our stewardship of creation. Care for the earth is a requirement of our faith. We are called to protect people and the planet, living our faith in relationship with all of God's creation. This environmental challenge has fundamental moral and ethical dimensions that cannot be ignored.

Dr. Paul
March 21, 2007

Blessed are the pure of heart: for they shall see God.

Matthew Ahr holding his brother Brian
(Photograph by Dr. Paul R. Ahr)

I have on my desk a photograph of my grandson Matthew, then just 3 years old, holding his newborn brother, Brian. When I think about being "pure of heart," my eyes and mind quickly scan in the direction of these two innocents. In many ways, this is an image I share with my old teacher and friend, Fr. Henri Nouwen who discusses the challenge of returning home and seeing God in his book, *The Return of the Prodigal Son*, as follows:

It is clear that the distance between turning around and the arrival at home needs to be traveled wisely and with discipline. The discipline is that of becoming a child of God. Jesus makes it clear that the way to God is the same as the way to a new childhood: "Unless you turn and become like little children you will never enter the Kingdom of Heaven." Jesus does not ask me to remain a child but to become one. Becoming a child is living toward a second innocence, not the innocence of the newborn infant, but the innocence reached through conscious choices.[24]

The journey home.

For Nouwen, the Beatitudes are a self-portrait of Jesus, and a map for each of us to get to our heavenly home, where we will be in the presence of God:

> The Beatitudes offer me the simplest route for the journey home, back into the house of my Father. And along this route, I will discover the joys of the second childhood: comfort, mercy, and an ever clearer vision of God. And as I reach home and feel the embrace of my Father, I will realize that not only heaven will be mine to claim, but that the earth as well will become my inheritance, a place where I can live in freedom without obsessions and compulsions.[25]

Seeing God on earth – especially at Camillus House.

Must we die "pure of heart" in order to see God in Heaven? I think not. To be "pure of heart" means to be able to set aside self-serving intentions and self-satisfying desires to perform selfless acts of service to others. Those who seek to see God on earth can be mindful of the lessons of Abraham and Lot (see pages 93-94) and the teachings of Sts. Macarius and Benedict (see pages 98-99) that God may appear to us in the form of a stranger or a pauper for whom we can perform the selfless acts Catholics know as the *Corporal* and *Spiritual Works of Mercy*:

Corporal Works of Mercy

- Feed the hungry
- Give drink to the thirsty
- Clothe the naked

Spiritual Works of Mercy

- Admonish the sinner
- Instruct the ignorant
- Counsel the doubtful

- Shelter the homeless
- Visit the imprisoned
- Visit the sick
- Bury the dead

- Comfort the sorrowful
- Bear wrongs patiently
- Forgive all injuries
- Pray for the living and the dead

Happily for our volunteers and staff, every day at Camillus House we perform the *Corporal Works of Mercy*. In the name of our benefactors we serve our brothers and sisters who present themselves as our guests. While we are ever hopeful that Christ is in our midst, perhaps disguised as a stranger or a pauper, we are privileged to see the greatness of God reflected in the goodness of these guests, each once a stranger, soon a friend.

Finally, under the spiritual guidance of the Brothers of the Good Shepherd, we perform the *Spiritual Works of Mercy* whenever we are provided the opportunity to do so. These acts especially include cautioning (i.e., admonishing) those whose addictions control their lives, instructing those who lack the knowledge to live productive and healthy lives and counseling and comforting those who are anxious and demoralized. Each day the Brothers pray for our benefactors and the special intentions that we bring to them, letting God see us and the things we seek from Him.

Dr. Paul
March 28, 2007

Blessed are the peacemakers: for they shall be called a child of God.

For most of my life, I have been a big proponent of peace. Growing up with four brothers, there seemed to be two kinds of peace. One was akin to being well-behaved. "Can we have some peace and quiet around here?" my father would sometimes bellow over the clamor of brothers tussling or taunting. Once I became a father that seemed like an exceptionally reasonable request.

The other was really BIG: the absence of war. "Peace on earth, good will to men" was for me a noble sentiment, especially when our country was at war, as it was during the Vietnam era. While in the US Navy in 1971, I had my passion for peace sorely tested when I was assigned to a three-person team that was to be parachuted into the demilitarized zone between North and South Vietnam as soon as a truce was declared there. The prospect of being thrown out of an airplane when peace broke out challenged my commitment to "peace on earth," not to mention "good will" to the senior officers who picked me to become the Department of Defense's hurling-toward-earth-at-a-great-rate-of-speed-praying-the-chute-will-open psychologist. Frankly, I never saw anything in household peace or worldwide peace to warrant being called a *child of God*.

Shalom

Preparing to recognize the ongoing financial support to Camillus House of our friend Edie Laquer last December prompted me to investigate the meanings of *shalom*, the Hebrew word for peace. When I did, I finally began to identify what kind of person could be called a *child of God*. Philip Birnbaum, in the *Encyclopedia of Jewish Concepts* defines *shalom* as follows: "The Hebrew word *shalom*...signifies welfare of every kind: security, contentment, sound health, prosperity, friendship, peace of mind and heart." [26] From this perspective, those who promote *shalom* are peace givers, peacemakers.

Peacemakers wanted.

It was then that I realized the extent to which what we do at Camillus House corresponds to shalom. Think about it: security, contentment, sound health, prosperity, friendship, peace of mind and heart.

- *Friendship?* Ask the 10,000 persons who receive a Camillus House service each year.

- *Security?* Ask the scores of persons who formerly "lived" on NE 1st Street, who now are provided a safe and caring place to sleep each night in our atrium and former parking lot. I have done just that. Two weeks after inviting people from the street to spend the night in our atrium and parking lot, Pat Cawley and I dropped in one night around 10 o'clock. Every person with whom we spoke thanked us for making these arrangements available because *they felt safer within our gates*. One man said he had not done drugs in ten nights because he was now safe from drug dealers who prey on people living on the street.

- *Sound health?* Ask the nearly 6,000 persons who are treated annually at Camillus Health Concern and the Camillus House Institute for Social and Personal Adjustment.

- *Prosperity?* Ask the 250 or so persons who receive GED training, job development, job training, and job placement services each year or the two ladies moving from homelessness into homes of their own.

- *Contentment?* Ask the recipients of the 400,000 free meals served at Camillus House each year.

- *Peace of mind and heart?* Ask the 800 – 900 persons (including nearly 180 children and 150 women) who spend the night under a Camillus House roof (or safely in our parking lot) *each night*, for a total of more than 300,000 no cost or low cost nights of shelter each year.

Thanks to the generosity of the more that 10,000 individuals, corporations and foundations who have contributed to Camillus House *so far in 2007*, these are all things that our volunteers and staff do every day in the Camillus organization through our Compassionate Hospitality, Comprehensive Healing, Career Help and Continuum of Housing programs. By their affiliation with Camillus House, our benefactors, volunteers and staff practice *shalom*, and thereby may be considered peace givers, peacemakers. As we plan for the expansion and upgrading of our shelter, meal and shower, treatment, vocational, and housing services at the new Camillus House and as we seek to raise more than $88 million to bring that plan to life, we reach out to the children of God to support us generously through their prayers, donated goods and services and financial support. *Shalom* to all who can be called *children of God*.

Dr. Paul
April 5, 2007

CHAPTER 7

I Was Poor and You Loved Me

The everyday practice of the Corporal Works of Mercy

(Letters from the 2008 Lent Season)

Forty Days and Counting

It seems that we have hardly gotten out of January, and here we are already in Lent 2008. I must admit, I long thought that *Lent* was an odd term to describe the 40+ days that precede Easter. When asked why this season was called *Lent*, a precocious schoolchild once told his catechism teacher that it was because "Jesus knew He was on *borrowed* time." Ash Wednesday should remind us that we, too, are on borrowed time.

At its root, our English word *Lent* has little to do with Easter or the 40 days leading up to it. In fact, our word has deviated dramatically from the Latin word that describes this season: *quadragesima*, or fortieth day. The integrity of this original meaning has been well preserved in many languages, for example, Spanish (*Cuaresma*) and French (*Carême*), but not English. The Germanic root of the English *Lent* refers to the season we call Spring, Yet as I watch weather reports from the Midwest and Northeast, I am sure that those who live there will be hard pressed to associate this time of year with Spring.

Corporal Works of Mercy.

This Lent I invite you to investigate with me the ways in which all of us who are Camillus House and Camillus Health Concern (Camillus) carry out what we call in our Catholic Christian tradition the *Corporal Works of Mercy*. The first six of these "works" are specifically listed in the Gospel of Matthew (25:34-40) as the criteria for admission into heaven. (The seventh – Bury the dead – was added in about the 3rd century.) Matthew quoted Jesus as follows:

Then the King will say to those at his right hand, 'Come, O blessed of my Father, inherit the kingdom prepared for you from the foundation of the world; for I was hungry and you gave me food [*feed the hungry*], I was thirsty and you gave me drink [*give drink to the thirsty*], I was a stranger and you welcomed me [*welcome the stranger*], I was naked and you clothed me [*clothe the naked*], I was sick and you visited me [*visit for the sick*], I was in prison and you came to me [*visit the imprisoned*].' Then the righteous will answer him, 'Lord, when did we see thee hungry and feed thee, or thirsty and give thee drink?' And the king will answer them, 'Truly, I say to you, as you did it to one of the least of my brethren, you did it to me' (Matthew 25:34-40).

Image of Divine Mercy originally painted under Sister Faustina's direction by Vilnius artist Eugene Kazimirowski in 1934.

Camillus House is a place full of mercy and a merciful place.

Beginning next week, we will reflect on each of these works of mercy in the context of the ways in which they define the work of Camillus as carried out each and every day by the Brothers of the Good Shepherd, our staff, volunteers and benefactors. On the last Thursday before Easter – Holy Thursday – we will see how the unfolding of Brother Mathias' gift to the people of Miami – Camillus House – has made present in this community a place where persons of good will can carry out our merciful God's will, as expressed by Jesus through Saint Faustina, the Apostle of Divine Mercy: "Tell ailing mankind to draw close to my merciful heart and I will fill them with peace."

On Holy Thursday two years ago (see page 133), incorporating the imagery of the Parable of the Prodigal Son, we reflected on the role that Camillus House plays in the gift of Divine Mercy, as follows:

> Camillus House is a plain on which our merciful God searches for and embraces His sons and daughters who seek to restore in their lives the good – the inherent dignity – that is their birthright. We celebrate our vocations as hosts and helpers, because when we reach out to these brothers and sisters as they seek to turn around or convert their lives, we comfort them as with the outstretched arms of Divine Mercy.

Over the next 40 days and 40 nights we will reflect on the ways in which we act as hosts and helpers. In short, we do it by carrying out (day in and day out) the *Corporal Works of Mercy*.

Dr. Paul
February 6, 2008

"...I was hungry and you gave me food, I was thirsty and you gave me drink..."

The ministry of the Brothers of the Good Shepherd in Miami began on August 20, 1960, when our founder, Brother Mathias Barrett, BGS, served meals of donated food and beverages to Cuban men living in public spaces near the Freedom Tower. Before Camillus House had been operational for three weeks, Hurricane Donna was sending her 150 mph winds across Miami-Dade County. Photos from that time show Brother Mathias

Brother Mathias Barrett is shown here welcoming individuals as they come to Camillus House for help nearly 50 years ago
(Source: Camillus House)

greeting long lines of hungry neighbors – some formerly homeless, others recently made homeless, and others with no place to get a meal – and offering the hospitality of the Brothers. For years, at the exact site of that original Camillus building – a rented house on NE 8th Street – we have maintained a large jug of cold water and disposable cups from which anyone could draw a refreshing drink at any time. Forty-seven years later, Camillus House is serving 500,000 free meals a year at our original downtown location and in Naranja.

We are not told to run a restaurant.

When Miami-Dade County residents were independently surveyed three years ago regarding their impressions of Camillus House, 94.8% of respondents stated that feeding persons who are homeless in Miami is the most important service that Camillus provides, and 45% stated that our meal program should remain our top priority. Despite this overwhelming community support, from time to time I encounter persons who believe that our meal programs are a disservice both to the community and to persons who are homeless. According to these critics, feeding persons who are poor and homeless *enables homelessness*. From this perspective, a gnawing hunger will motivate a person who is homeless to work or else to move on to another place where he or she can find a meal, any meal.

Come spend just part of a day with me at our Courtyard program, now an integral part of our main shelter operation. Here you will find men and (now increasingly more) women, some of whom work but cannot earn enough money to secure and pay for an inexpensive room or apartment. Many more of them – those who are chronically homeless – have long-term physical and/or mental disabilities or powerful addictions and are currently unemployable. These special persons are poor in so many ways: economically poor, in poor health, in poor spirits, with a poor prognosis. Alienated from family, abandoned by friends and marginalized by society, their horizons are as short as dead-end alleys and, except for Camillus, their next meal could likely come from a dumpster. These persons are our guests.

Then-Bishop Coleman Carroll is shown here carving a turkey at Camillus House in 1961. The year before, he had asked Brother Mathias Barrett and the Brothers of the Good Shepherd to help by providing services to the growing number of Cuban immigrants arriving in Miami at the time.

(Source: Camillus House)

The gospels do not call upon us to run a restaurant, to serve those who have the means to pay for their meals and pay for their drinks. We are

– 165 –

not told to "run a tab" for those who we expect to pay us back when they get a good job. We are told to feed the hungry and give drink to the thirsty with no prospect of recompense in this life. And that is what we do, and in doing so we *enable human dignity*.

The transforming charity of our benefactors and volunteers.

And as we do it, we see the transforming power of the charity of our benefactors and volunteers. We see men and women who are homeless begin to realize that *they are not hopeless*. We see individuals who are trapped in the isolation that leads to and follows from living on the streets set aside the ways of the street and sit and eat and sleep and socialize alongside each other. We see the generosity of our benefactors and the hospitality of the Brothers and our staff coax out of persons who have lived on the street their inherent humanity, often long held from public view. We see persons who have been street homeless aspire to break their personal cycles of homelessness, and by seeking medical care, rehabilitation and job training, achieve it.

To the corporations and individuals who donate food and juice and coffee and to the hundreds of volunteers who help us feed the hungry and give drink to the thirsty by participating in our casserole program through their local parishes or by bringing other prepared meals to our main shelter, or by serving in our food line, thank you for all that you do for those persons who are poor and homeless in Miami. Today is the Feast of St. Valentine, and everywhere we look – from paper cups to boxer shorts to fancy candy boxes – we are surrounded by bright red hearts signifying love. Everyday at Camillus House we are surrounded by the Camillus heart signifying the love reciprocated between our benefactors, volunteers and staff and our guests and clients. Happy St. Valentine's Day!

Dr. Paul
February 14, 2008

"...I was a stranger and you welcomed me, I was naked and you clothed me ..."

In the early 1970s, our founder, Brother Mathias Barrett, BGS wrote to Miami Archbishop Coleman Carroll. In his letter, Brother Mathias described his dream to establish at Camillus House a program where eight (8) "men of the road could be sheltered and cared for during the day, as well as at night." On Tuesday, nearly 1,000 men, women and children spent the night in a Camillus facility and not on the streets of Miami-Dade County. We sometimes imagine Brother Mathias returning to Camillus House, jokingly wondering whether he would tell us: "Well done good and faithful servants," or "I only said *eight* men." The Brothers assure us that our founder would be especially proud of all that the benefactors, volunteers and staff have been able to accomplish for the men, women and children of Miami who are poor and homeless.

We are building a system of care and a continuum of housing.

When Brother Mathias established Camillus House he founded this ministry with a motto and a goal: *Charity Unlimited*. Today we shelter and care for: (a) over 250 persons in our Courtyard program that allows *anyone* to come and live with us at our main shelter; (b) approximately 80 men who are receiving substance abuse, mental illness and/or physical health treatment; (c) approximately 65 men who receive free room and board while they search for a job and/or a place to live; (d) transitional housing for 130 single persons and 40 families; and (e) permanent housing for 74 single persons and 57 families. Over the next year, we will add a seven (7) apart-

Brother Bill Osmanski of the Brothers of the Good Shepherd is shown here assisting a Camillus House client with his clothing needs.
(Photograph by Gina Fontana)

ment program for young men aging out of foster care and a new 90-bed apartment program due South of our Somerville Residence, which is visible from Interstate 95 in downtown Miami. Finally, in 2010 we will be replacing our main shelter with a new 340-bed state-of-the-art Camillus House Center near the Jackson Hospital complex. Our long-term goal is to own/operate facilities that will provide dignified housing for 1,600 men, women and children who were homeless or at serious risk of becoming homeless in Miami-Dade County.

I was naked and you *showered* and *clothed* me.

For many years, Camillus House has provided the opportunity for men and women who are homeless in Miami to get a shower and clean clothes. When I first came to Camillus House in 2004, homeless women were able to get a shower one day a week. We quickly changed that, and now women who are homeless in Miami can get a shower three days a week and a change of clothing as needed. We rely heavily on clothing donations from throughout the Miami community to allow us to provide clean clothes to anyone who requests them. Groups such as our Camillus House Young

Leaders (CHYL) routinely hold clothing drives to provide us with new underwear and cotton socks. Last Thanksgiving, CHYL Board member Jimmy Torres presented 5,500 pairs of new boxer shorts and 3,000 pairs of new socks donated by his fellow employees at City Furniture. The entrance fee for the most recent Camillus staff Christmas party was two pairs of new underwear.

According to Brother Bill Osmanski, Brother Mathias had a special concern for women who were homeless, exhorting the Brothers to "take care of my ladies." He often took money from his own pocket to pay for lodging in an inexpensive motel so that homeless women could have a few nights of peaceful rest off the streets. The wish of our founder has become the focus of the charitable giving of Board member Sue Gallagher and her husband Doug through the Women's Fund of Mimi-Dade, and the work of one of our most regular volunteers: Jodi Dickinson. Jodi has lovingly converted our rather ordinary women's shower program into an extraordinary ministry that brings to life the Brothers' charism of *respect for human dignity*. Through her week-in and week-out presence at the shower program, and the little touches that she brings to it – music, candles, books and perfumes – Jodi has also transformed her personal service to *Brother Mathias' ladies* from an avocation to a vocation. Happily for the persons we serve, Jodi is but one of scores of volunteers who routinely practice the Corporal Works of Mercy in and through Camillus House, for which we are all very grateful.

Dr. Paul
February 21, 2008

"...I was sick and you visited me ..."

*N*urse Kate Callahan loves the poor. I know this because Kate Callahan, R.N. regularly takes time from her work as a principal at the Huntington Consulting Group to volunteer for Camillus Health Concern (CHC) and Camillus House (CH) at our main shelter. *Doctor* Kate Callahan loves the poor. I know this because Kate Callahan, Ph.D. has also served as a Member of the CH Board of Directors, and currently serves as Chairwoman of the CHC Board. Kate is one of several health care professionals who routinely carry out this Corporal Work of Mercy by volunteering on site, or in their offices, for Camillus Health Concern and Camillus House's Institute for Social and Personal Adjustment (CH-ISPA).

Camillus Health Concern.

Founded in 1984 by the legendary Dr. Pedro Jose "Joe" Greer, Jr., Brother Paul Johnson, BGS and volunteers such as Rose Anderson, ARNP, Alina Perez-Stable, MSW and others, CHC has been a leader in providing primary health care services to persons who are poor and homeless in Miami-Dade County for nearly a quarter century. CHC has been a Health Care for the Homeless grantee through the Department of Health and Human Services' Bureau of Primary Health Care since 1989 and was designated as a Federally Qualified Health Center in 1996. CHC's Board of Directors is 51% consumer-based, which strengthens all clinical, operational and programmatic processes.

CHC services are provided at 336 NW 5th Street in downtown Miami. Opened in June of 1998, the state-of-the-art health center offers persons who are homeless the opportunity to receive quality care in a professional and comfortable setting. Primary health care services are provided at three community sites in addition to the Camillus main shelter: Better Way of Miami; the Salvation Army; and the shelter established by Mother Teresa of Calcutta and operated by her Sisters of Charity. Patients are referred from these sites to the main center as needed.

Camillus Health Concern RN Isabel Hill shares a light moment with one of her patients who is homeless.
(Photograph by Gina Fontana)

CHC's tri-lingual (English, Spanish and Creole) staff of 45 are specially trained in meeting the unique health care and social service needs of persons who are homeless, and provide high quality medical services under the clinical direction of Rosendo Collazo, D.O., Director of Health Services for CHC and CH and the administrative leadership of Hirut Kassaye, MPH. Annually, CHC provides over 24,000 visits to more than 5,200 clients.

Institute for Social and Personal Adjustment.

Substance abuse problems and untreated mental illnesses are two of the primary causes of chronic homelessness. Most persons who are homeless experience both of these conditions, as well as suffer from serious and persistent medical conditions. Recognizing that addictions and mental illness are diseases – not choices, at Camillus House we provide treatment so that clients can overcome these conditions and return to being productive members of our society. With an 89% success rate, ISPA is considered one of the most effective programs of its kind in the nation.

Growing out of the pioneering work of Brother Harry Somerville, BGS with men who were homeless and substance dependent in the 1980s, ISPA was redesigned in 1997 as a comprehensive program treating mental illness and substance abuse by Patricia Cawley, LCSW, BCD, CH's current Chief Operating Officer. Under the clinical and administrative direction of Kathy Garcia, LMHC, ISPA is licensed for outpatient, day/night, residential, and aftercare services, and includes components for family therapy, wellness, relapse prevention, and coordination with medical care. A psychiatrist provides psychiatry services and monitors medications. A relationship with Jackson Memorial Hospital ensures that clients are able to obtain all of their medications for free. Outpatient services are provided on the campus of the Homeless Assistance Center in Homestead, FL. Annually, ISPA graduates 70 men who were formerly homeless to productive lives no longer dominated by their addictions and/or mental illness.

In addition to residential substance abuse and mental health treatment services, ISPA offers outreach, case management, outpatient, and day center services, temporary housing assistance through our homeless prevention program. HIV/AIDS prevention and treatment services are provided in conjunction with CHC.

Dr. Paul
February 28, 2008

"...I was constrained and you helped me become free..."

Several months ago, staff of Camillus Health Concern and Camillus House attended the funeral of Lourdes Collazo-Harris, sister of Dr. Ross Collazo and cousin of Alina Perez-Stable. It was a wonderful celebration of her life, held in the beautiful Church of St. John Neumann.[27] While in the vestibule, I noticed that the *Corporal Works of Mercy* were engraved along the walls. As my eye crossed over the list, my glance was halted when I read: *Ransom the captive* where I was expecting *Visit the imprisoned*. I recalled the "ransom" terminology from my youth, and began to think about which of these exhortations best fit the ministry of the Brothers of the Good Shepherd in Miami and the Mission of Camillus House.

The evolving opportunities for *mercy*.

In the early and Medieval Christian Church, both visiting those who were imprisoned and ransoming those held captive were important charitable acts. Many early Christians, including St. Peter, were imprisoned for their faith. During the Crusades (1095-1270), Christian pilgrims were kidnapped and held for ransom by highway robbers along the way and by their adversaries in the Holy Land. In fact, during the height of the Crusades, several religious orders were established for the primary purpose of ransoming captive pilgrims.[28]

To help resolve the matter of which terminology best describes Camillus' role in our times, I met with Father David Russell who, as the Pastor of

St. John Neumann parish, was responsible for the design and construction of this spectacular church. We spoke in general regarding our Christian responsibility to visit those imprisoned, especially since one percent of the US population are incarcerated, with African-Americans and Hispanics being over-represented among prison inmates. As we spoke, our thinking converged on a more contemporary focus for this Work of Mercy, which might be best titled: *I was constrained and you helped me become free.*

"Man is born free, but everywhere he is in chains."

This observation by the 18th century French philosopher Jean Jacques Rousseau underscores the breadth of opportunity available to persons of good will who agree with the challenge tentatively identified in my conversation with Father Russell. It is repeated in John O'Donohue's book, *Eternal Echoes* in the chapter provocatively titled "Prisons we choose to

(Source: iStockphoto)

live in." Pat Cawley tells me that when she conducted meditation sessions with our treatment clients using this chapter as a focus, the results were very powerful.

Every day at Camillus we meet and are met by persons who are constrained – perhaps even confined – by their medical conditions, their mental illnesses and addictions, their illiteracy and inadequate education, and their unemployability and poverty. Thanks to the generosity of our benefactors and the availability of public funding, we are able to help our brothers and sisters free themselves from these constraints, without regard for the source of their problems. We provide the highest quality medical treatment, addictions and mental illness treatment, GED preparation, job training and placement in the fields of warehouse and transportation, food and beverage and other hospitality careers to loosen the bonds of self-imprisonment and help the persons who come to us as our guests and participate with us as our clients become productive citizen-graduates. More than visiting them through our hospitality and availability, the financial support of our bene-factors helps us – together – to "ransom" these "captives" in real and socially beneficial ways and helps them to replenish their self-esteem and recapture their dignity.

Dr. Paul
March 6, 2008

To bury the dead.

Once again we touch on the theme of dying, death and our obligations to those who have died. Over the past year we have said goodbye to ones close to us such as: Annette Jackson; Ross Collazo's sister; Tina Solis' sister; Deidra Cesar's brother; Carmen Arias' father; Karen Hursey-McLaughlin's father; Jenner Pierre's grandfather; Michelle Rodriguez' grandmother; Aaron Peoples' grandmother and many clients/friends who have lived with us. Earlier this month, we were especially saddened by the death of Dinora Caballero who was often seen at our Somerville Residence in her wheelchair being cared for by her mother Nubia. We continue to hold these persons close to our hearts as we recall the things of value that they have contributed to our lives.

The origins of this Corporal Work of Mercy.

While the first six Corporal Works of Mercy constitute guidance from Christ Himself on how to gain entrance into the Kingdom of Heaven, this seventh Work of Mercy was added by Church leaders in the third century. This was a time when early Christians were hunted down and murdered, sometimes for sport and the bodies of many Christian martyrs were thrown into the streets to decay. Fellow Christians were encouraged to provide their dead with proper Christian burials, sometimes at a risk to their own safety.

These early Christians were influenced in their reverence for the dead by the actions and writings of Tobias (or Tobit), a devout and wealthy Israelite living among the captives deported to Nineveh from the northern kingdom of Israel in 721 B.C. The autobiographical Old Testament Book of Tobias 1:16-18 recalls his many "charitable works for my kinsmen and my people," especially these which preview the works of mercy listed by Christ more than seven centuries later: "I would give my bread to the hungry and my clothing to the naked. If I saw one of my people who had died and been thrown outside the walls of Nineveh, I would bury him." Tobias was particularly noted for his diligence in providing proper burials for fallen Israelites slain by King Sennacherib, who seized all Tobias' property and exiled him for carrying out these burials.

Too much of a good thing?

Thanks to the generosity of Paul Johnson, the former CEO of Camillus House and now Director of Cemeteries for the Archdiocese of Miami,

Camillus has the use of a section of a mausoleum for the entombment of the ashes of persons who are formerly homeless. The Brothers of the Good Shepherd diligently and reverently conduct memorial services for persons who have died in our care or for other persons who are homeless and are known to us.

But as we have become more and more familiar with more and more persons who have been living on the streets of Miami and now spend their days and nights at our Courtyard, we have begun

(Source: iStockphoto)

to pay closer attention to those among us who are dying tragic and lonely deaths due to drug use. Here is an excerpt from an email I received last month from Jodi Dickinson regarding the death of "Tanya," a regular participant in our women's shower program:

> I asked where "Tanya" was today, (she was my go-to-girl). She was always honest and upfront with me. I came to trust her, as well as rely on her for help and information regarding the women. She is dead, from an overdose of heroin. She overdosed in Gibson Park. I spoke to the woman who was with her when this occurred.

Unhappily, too many "Tanyas" and "Tonys" and other vulnerable people in this community are being *prayed over* by the Brothers and other persons of good will – those who deal in hope – after being *preyed upon* by drug dealers who sell them the means to kill themselves – those who deal in dope. It is right that we reverently bury our homeless dead whose bodies might otherwise be left on the streets to decay like the victims of Sennacherib or the early Christian martyrs. But it would be far better for us to do everything in our power to feed and shelter and clothe and treat and rehabilitate these gentle folk and to ransom them from the captivity of their mental and physical illnesses and addictions, so that we may have them grow old with us. And then when they reach the full limits of their lives, we should arrange for a proper and reverential burial of their bodies as their souls return to the house of our Father.

Dr. Paul
March 13, 2008

To love the poor.

Today is Holy Thursday, the eve of the day on which our Savior *voluntarily* redeemed humanity with the gift of His life. Brother Bill Osmanski, BGS often reminds us that our founder, Brother Mathias, counted on the generosity of volunteers to carry out God's work through Camillus House. "I don't expect us to be too large of a congregation," Brother Bill remembers Brother Mathias saying, "but I do expect that we will do great things for God and the Church. We must rely on our volunteers to follow in our steps and to love the poor."

Twelve who love the poor.

Fred Peel is our longest serving volunteer. For 18 years, Fred has been coming to Camillus House to assist in the kitchen, mail room and staff offices. Anywhere Camillus House is short-handed, Fred is there to help. Next month, Fred will be awarded the *Presidential Volunteer Service Award*. This award was created by the President's Council on Service and Civic Participation, which was established by President George W. Bush in 2003.

Every week, twice a week, for four years **Magdalena Murillo** comes to the Camillus House administration building to help with office work. It's not glamorous work, but Magdalena regularly assists the accounting department review files, organize receipts, and do the little things that help our overall operation.

Almost every morning you can find **Odessa Cruess** in the Camillus House kitchen preparing the silverware for the day's meals. Odessa, who

For many years, the Pedro family has opened their hearts to the poor by providing and serving meals to those in need every week at Camillus House. During one of their recent visits to Camillus, Tony and Janette Pedro along with their daughter Yohana took a moment for this photo.

(Photograph by Frank Ferrara)

is in her mid-70s, got involved with Camillus House through AARP. She is at Camillus House every week and has become a surrogate mother for volunteers and ISPA clients who work in the kitchen.

Every Thursday night after he closes his electronics store in downtown Miami, **Tony Pedro** heads to Camillus House. Chances are his wife **Janette Pedro** is already there. With their own money, Tony, Janette and their family prepare and serve a fantastic meal that feeds both the bodies and the spirits of those who accept our invitation to dinner.

Visitors to our dining rooms frequently comment on the fresh cut flowers in vases on every dining table. At every meal at Camillus House there are fresh flowers at every table. For the past three years, these flowers have been a gift from florist **Shirley Brodsky** who enjoys adding a sense of normality and dignity for Camillus House guests who won't find that atmosphere on the streets.

Thanksgiving and Christmas are two of the biggest days of the year at Camillus House and every year, veterinarian **Barry Mitzner** of Kendall is there to help organize the hundreds of volunteers who want to serve and the hundreds of guests being served on those days.

Dr. Carl Lowell and the clients of Camillus have a reason to smile. Dr. Lowell is proud of his son, Boston Red Sox 3rd baseman Mike, who was selected *Most Valuable Player* for the 2007 Major League Baseball World Series. When he is not rooting for Mike or taking care of his private patients, this Coral Gables dentist comes to Camillus Health Concern once a month to provide for the dental care needs of persons who are poor and homeless in Miami.

Physical therapy can be a long and difficult process, often unavailable to persons who are poor and homeless. That is why Camillus Health Concern is lucky to have Jackson Memorial Hospital Physical Therapists **Kadima Dean**, **Carmen Romero**, and **Judy Humelberg** volunteer at our clinic. For years they have been helping clients who wouldn't otherwise be able to see a physical therapist, making sure the healing process is complete.

Coral Gables Attorney **Christi Sherouse** donates her time and efforts as head of the Camillus House Young Leaders (aka CHYL), a group of young Miami professionals dedicated to supporting Camillus House. Christi spearheads efforts that include volunteer projects, fundraising events, and donation drives as well as raising awareness of Camillus House within the next generation of Miami's leaders.

Happy Easter to every one of our volunteers, benefactors and staff and to your families!

Dr. Paul
March 20, 2008

CHAPTER 8

This Is What We Do

Reflections on the experience of being homeless

(Letters from the 2009 Lent Season)

Signs, plaques and banners.

Today is Ash Wednesday 2009. When my sons Tom and Andy were pre-schoolers, the music of *Sesame Street* filled our house for hours each day. One of their favorite songs was *X Marks the Spot*, two lines of which still reverberate in my head: *'X' marks the spot. 'X' stands for danger.* Today, many Christians will have a mark placed on our foreheads – in the shape of a **✝**, not an **✗**, that will serve as a reminder of our own mortality, and a sign to others of our Christian faith.

Mounted at the entrance to our main shelter there is another sign, a plaque really, that was inspired by this sign atop the gates of Hell in Dante's *Inferno*: "Abandon hope all who enter here." Our plaque reverses this image:

Photograph by Gina Fontana

For the persons who enter our gates, especially those whose stay in our Courtyard represents their first step to breaking their own cycle of homelessness, the words on this plaque represent our enduring pledge to help them on their quest through the gifts of hope, dignity, healing and community. This Lent, we will elaborate on these four gifts, each meant to augment the five *charisms* of the Brothers of the Good Shepherd: respect for human dignity, availability, hospitality, flexibility and adaptability.

Next week we will address one of the most basic needs of persons who live on the streets of Miami or any community: freedom from fear. We will describe the fullness of fear experienced "on the street" by persons who are our guests and clients, and the ways that we replace fear with hope. We will see that for many persons who are homeless, security and acceptance allows them to begin their personal transformation from homelessness to hopefulness. In our third letter, we will reflect on the ways in which life on the street diminishes the dignity and sense of self-worth of persons who are homeless, and how Camillus helps them regain human dignity both in their own eyes and in the eyes of others.

In the week that includes the Feast of St. Patrick, we will review the life of another Irish Saint: St. Dymphna, patroness of persons who suffer from a mental illness. We will also reflect on the life of St. John of God, patron of and founder of the Order of Hospitallers. Brother Mathias Barrett, BGS, founder of the Congregation of the Little Brothers of the Good Shepherd and of Camillus House began his religious life at age 16 when he entered the Hospitaller Order of St. John of God. Reflections on the lives of these holy role models will prepare us to address during the following week the role that Camillus Health Concern and Camillus House play in healing the bodies, minds and spirits of persons who seek our care.

In the next-to-last week, we will investigate the loneliness that comes with living on the street and the ways in which persons who are homeless cope – sometimes successfully, sometimes not – with that loneliness. Finally, on Holy Thursday we will reflect on and give thanks for the many ways in which Camillus House and Camillus Health Concern promote hope, dignity and healing to all who come to us as strangers at our gate, and become part of our community.

As we make plans to relocate from our NE 1st Avenue site to our new home on NW 7th Avenue, we realize that we will be leaving behind many of the physical components of our half-century of work on NE 1st Avenue. But we will bring this plaque with us, and once remounted at our new home, it will serve as a reminder – a sign – to ourselves and to others for our next 50 years in Miami that we have the privilege to participate in the Brothers' ministry of hope, dignity, healing and community.

Dr. Paul
February 25, 2009

Abandon fear all who enter here; we offer you hope.

Some readers may find it peculiar for me to be writing about the fear experienced *by* persons who are homeless rather than a fear *of* persons who are homeless. In the 28 years since I first worked with persons who were homeless in St. Louis, I have been struck by the extent to which fear is a constant companion of persons who live on the streets of any city. Here, I want to describe some aspects of *this* fear.

Fear of harm and loss.

Before we ever thought of opening the Camillus Courtyard to all adult persons who are homeless in Miami-Dade County, I had directed that "stadium style" lights and surveillance cameras be installed on three sides of our Main Shelter building. I had hoped that the bright lights would encourage the persons camping out there every night to move to another location. My concern was that the driver of a large truck lumbering up NE 1st Avenue toward the Interstate 95 on-ramp might get distracted or otherwise lose control, striking some or all of the persons sleeping there. To my surprise, the 40 or so persons who had long been sleeping on our sidewalk did not believe that I wanted them to move at all. Rather, they saw the lights and cameras, undeservedly, as a sign of our compassionate concern for their well-being there, having been installed near the time of the beatings of homeless men in Ft. Lauderdale. In short, they saw our actions as an invitation to them to stay, and within days the number of persons sleeping on our side of the street nearly doubled, with many women now living on our sidewalk for the first time.

I learned three important lessons in this exchange. First, persons who are homeless tend to stay awake at night and sleep in well-trafficked places during the day (a situation that we had inadvertently created on NE 1st Avenue). Second, a place that provides personal safety will attract and retain persons who are homeless. Third, persons who are homeless will thank you (and sometimes bless you) for perceived kindnesses to them, even if it was not your intent to be kind to them.

Clifford Petit-Homme, Day Center Supervisor for Camillus House, offers hope to an individual who is homeless by inviting him to come into the organization's shelter.

(Photograph by Gina Fontana)

Persons who are homeless remain vigilant 24 hours a day. "Certain places you wouldn't eat from," reports William, once homeless and now residing with us, "[some people] might poison you." "A homeless person has got to be ready to go at the spur of the moment" Emmett, another man who was once homeless adds. "I had the fear of being attacked, I was afraid of somebody taking the little bit of stuff I had" relates Angel, a third formerly homeless man.

Fear of an *inner death*.

Fear of harm, of arrest, of losing all one's earthly possessions are real and, in a strange way, life affirming. For some persons who live on the street, there is a fear of no longer being able to be afraid; a fear of giving up and giving in to an all-consuming fear: hopelessness. Camillus House's Institute of

Social and Personal Adjustment (CH-ISPA) Director Kathy Garcia speaks of an *inner death* experienced by many persons who are street homeless. For Kathy, this inner death is a feeling of spiritual depletion or hopelessness that leads its victims to give up on trying and living. "I laid back on the street and looked at other people," William told me, "I wondered, *Was this it? I might as well just lay down and die. Am I ever going to change? Maybe I should walk out on Biscayne Boulevard and let a truck hit me.*" Angel echoed William's hopelessness: "I used to ask myself, *Is this going to [continue to] be the same for me?*" For these men, at that time, *inner death* had begun to overtake their lives.

When fear subsides, hope can advance.

Fear subsides in the presence of familiarity, especially a familiarity that helps one feel safe. For a person living on the street, the fear associated with, for example, scavenging food or catching a few hours of fitful sleep is reduced when conducted at a place that is familiar and perceived to be safe. Add genuine and predictable security and genuine and predictable hospitality, such as we offer in the Camillus Courtyard, and hope advances as fear subsides.

This does not take place in a night or a week, perhaps not even a month or two or three. But as our sidewalk-lighting experience taught us, a predictably fear-less place, a place of safety, draws persons from a life on the street and, as long as we keep them safe, holds them long enough for them to glimpse – and often grasp – the spirit of hopefulness that breaks the cycle of homelessness.

Dr. Paul
March 5, 2009

Abandon shame all who enter here; we offer you dignity.

During last week's interviews on the subject of fear, Angel, Ivan, William and Marshall (aka Emmett) discussed another source of fear while being homeless: the fear of encountering persons whom you know – especially family members or friends from one's pre-homeless life.

Shame and stigma.

From the point of view of the person who is homeless, this sense of shame is closely associated with, and maybe even powered by, negative reactions to strangers who are shoddily dressed or otherwise unkempt. These reactions, based on stereotypes and labels, are a form of stigma. William shares his feeling of shame while homeless:

> It was shame by me to let you know I was homeless. If you know I was homeless you would down-rate me; treat me like I am on the bottom of the earth. I would want to be treated like anyone else. Most of the time you would see that I was homeless because of how I was dressed.

Such stereotypes engender wariness, and sometimes fear, in ordinary citizens. According to Angel, "When I came into a store, [people] were afraid of me, like I was going to rob the store."

You cannot look in the looking glass.

Such stereotypes influence the self-perceptions and self-esteem of persons who are homeless. In his groundbreaking essay, *Eight Ages of Man*, psychoanalyst Erik Erikson discusses shame as follows:

> Shame is an emotion insufficiently studied, because in our civilization it is so early and easily absorbed by guilt. Shame supposes that one is completely exposed and conscious of being looked at: in one word, self-conscious. One is visible and not ready to be visible...Shame is early expressed in an impulse to bury one's face, or to sink, right then and there, into the ground.

A jubilant group of graduates of Camillus' ISPA treatment program celebrate their accomplishment.

(Photograph by Gina Fontana)

For many persons who are homeless, a mirror is a painful reminder of their amplified self-consciousness and diminished self-esteem. They routinely cast their eyes away from their reflection in a store window or a mirror. "You try to avoid mirrors," admits William, who adds that otherwise, "you'd be very much ashamed." According to Camillus COO Pat Cawley, progress in treatment, whether for substance abuse or mental illness, can often be tracked by a client's increased attention to his/or her appearance and willingness to risk looking into a mirror to measure progress toward his/her normal appearance.

Shedding shame, donning dignity.

For many men and women who are homeless *and* substance abusers, drugs and/or alcohol help them to stop feeling badly about themselves. The opportunity to share their drugs and/or booze with others, that is, *to party*, helps them feel *more than* good about themselves: "you feel like the King of the World," Godfrey relates. The unconditional positive regard shown to new guests and clients by Camillus staff accelerates the transition from the false self-esteem offered by drugs and alcohol, to a more enduring self-esteem based on unveiling each man's and each woman's inherent human dignity. Others who have a mental illness or are merely displaced share in the enhanced self-esteem that is a by-product of that caring.

Good food, the opportunity to rest, the presence of others making the same passage from shame to dignity, and the availability of caring staff to guide the way accelerate the journey. One of the first stops on the transformation from shame to self-esteem is the ability, according to Godfrey, to "see the person in the mirror who you [formerly] were," which comes after "a couple of weeks eating good and getting sleep." And, the caring. For William, "Camillus House makes you feel that you are part of society. You are family and they love you." Marshall offers: "You give us a sense of responsibility. We're back in charge of our life." "You put the dignity in us," William echoes.

"No," we reply, "we help you find where you misplaced it, and help you put it on."

Dr. Paul
March 12, 2009

Our Saints are Mindful of Our Needs

Persons who we would identify as suffering from a physical or mental illness have long relied on the charity of family, friends and strangers and the intercession of Saints to make their way peacefully through the world. Two Catholic Saints have been recognized for their dedication to the needs of persons who are physically or mentally ill.

Patroness of persons with a mental illness.

By the 7th Century A.D., most of Ireland had been converted to Christianity, although some pagan sects continued, and inter-marriage was not uncommon. Dymphna was the child of such a union, the daughter of Damon, a petty king or chieftain and a Christian woman of noble heritage. Mother and daughter were renowned for their physical beauty and devout Christianity.

Saint Dymphna
(Source: Catholic Online)

When Dymphna was a teenager, her mother died, and she and her father were inconsolable in their grief. To assuage his grief, Damon sent forth his courtiers to find a woman who matched his beloved wife in beauty and grace. Upon their return, his agents admitted that only Dymphna was as beautiful and kind as his late wife and that he should marry his daughter. Taking their advice, Damon set out to convince 15-year old Dymphna to participate in this dark plan. She resisted, and ultimately fled with her priest counselor, Father Gerebran to the Continent. Damon pursued them to the town of Gheel, Belgium where Damon confronted them. He beheaded Saint Gerebran on the spot, and when Dymphna rebuffed his offer of marriage, he also killed her in a rage.

The bodies of the Dymphna and her confessor were buried by the local people, and eventually a shrine to St. Dymphna was built there. Gradually, persons with serious mental illnesses were brought by the families or traveled by themselves to pray at that shrine. Many experienced miraculous recoveries from their illnesses, and the reputation of the shrine and its healing powers spread far and wide. Eventually, there were so many pilgrims to the site that local families in this rural farming community began to provide room and board to those pilgrims who did not enjoy a speedy miraculous cure in exchange for help around the farm. Many mental health professionals credit the personal and tender care provided to persons with a mental illness by generations of Gheel families with accelerating their return to a normal life. The first American application of the Gheel foster family care program was begun 40 years ago in rural New Haven, Missouri with similar beneficial results. The Gheel approach has since been replicated throughout the United States and the world, and the personal and tender care offered in our Courtyard is modeled on the kindness still offered by the citizens of Gheel.

March 8th is a special day.

João Cidade was born in Montemor-o-Novo, Portugal on March 8, 1495. As a young man, João worked as a shepherd, and later served as a soldier under Holy Roman Emperor Charles V. As an adult, he is said to have had a vision of the Infant Jesus, who gave him the name *John of God* and directed him to go to Granada. There he experienced a major spiritual conversion while listening to a sermon by St. John of Ávila, the man who would later become his spiritual mentor.

Saint John of God
(Source: Wikimedia Commons)

João distributed all his possessions to the poor of the city, and went through Granada publicly calling on God for mercy and forgiveness of his sins. The townsfolk thought him to be mad, and he was confined to the local madhouse. He recovered after a visit from his spiritual mentor, and subsequently dedicated himself to the care and treatment of the poorest and neediest of his fellow citizens. He rented a small house where he cared for the sick, begging supplies at night and caring for his charges during the day. In time, he attracted a small band of companions who formed the nucleus of the Order of Hospitallers, now better known as the Brothers Hospitallers of St. John of God, who care for the sick in countries around the world. Brother Mathias, BGC, the founder of Camillus House and of the Congregation of the Little Brothers of the Good Shepherd began his life as a Religious as a Brother in the Hospitaller Order of St. John of God and served with distinction in the Hospitaller's ministries in Europe, Canada and the United States.

St. John of God died on March 8, 1550 – his 55th birthday – mere weeks before the birth of the man with whom he shares the distinction of being named the Patron Saint of the sick and of nurses: St. Camillus de Lellis.

Dr. Paul
March 19, 2009

Abandon hurt all who enter here; we offer you healing.

Before and above all things, care must be taken of the sick, that they be served in very truth as Christ is served, because He hath said, "I was sick and you visited Me" (Mathew 25:36). And "as long as you did it to one of these My least brethren, you did it to Me" (Mathew 25:40). But let the sick themselves also consider that they have served for the honor of God, and let them not grieve their brethren who serve them by unnecessary demands. These must, however, be patiently borne with, because from such as these a more bountiful reward is gained. Let the Abbot's greatest concern, therefore, be that they suffer no neglect.

– The Rule of St. Benedict Chapter XXXVI: Of the Sick Brethren.

The Rule of St. Benedict, written in about 530 A.D., concisely summarizes the Gospel injunction to care for sick persons. Last Lent (February 28, 2008) we reviewed the excellent physical health, mental health and substance abuse treatment programs provided by Camillus Health Concern (CHC) and Camillus House's Institute of Social and Personal Adjustment (ISPA). Since its establishment in January 2007, the Camillus Courtyard has been a major portal of entry into our health, mental health and substance abuse services, and for the past two years, Camillus Health Concern has staffed a full service clinic at Camillus' main shelter. RNs, ARNPs and physicians serve patients in our medical respite beds and provide ambulatory care to Courtyard clients and guests.

Life on the streets is an unhealthy life.

When you live on the street, Marshall tells us," if you're hurt or you're sick, you bear with it. It's a miserable feeling. You have to live with the aches and pains." When the hurt hurts too much, Mike says, "you call 911. I broke my foot doing an odd painting job and had to walk on it for two days until it got too bad. Then I called 911." Angel observes that, "when you are homeless, you're more likely to get sick. You're laying down in places where people have gotten sick or worse. Doctors don't want to see you because you have

Shelter nurse Patricia Forde and residential assistant, Ralph Clark (left) meet with a Camillus client.

no insurance. When you're on the street you develop a *don't care* attitude." Shelter-based nursing staff report that once under our care, Courtyard guests and clients report serious and chronic medical conditions that they never experienced before, perhaps because they self-medicated with drugs or alcohol while living on the streets.

Healing body, mind *and* spirit.

The most outstanding feature of our staff is their *concern* for our patients, clients and guests. Mike, who is in a respite bed, credits Dr. Hiriart and the other medical staff for the comprehensiveness and competence of their caring:

When you hit her door the nurse asks, "How are you feeling today? Have you had this [test or procedure] done?" They don't focus on one perspective. Pat [Forde] went out of her way; she went to Fred [Mims] and went the extra mile to make sure I got into [substance abuse] treatment. She remembered I had a Court date. They remember what you tell them. Even if you don't want the help, they'll push it. There is a lot of compassion. They spend time with you.

Medical staff, ISPA staff, Courtyard staff and especially the Brothers are lauded for their competence, availability, flexibility and concern. "Father Sam looks like he never goes home. I always see him talking with the homeless," Angel reports. The same sentiments are related about Brother Bill and Brother Charles. "All Mr. Mims has to do is walk through [the Courtyard] and he'll have 100 people to talk to," Angel adds. William says, "You have staff you can talk to who help you relax your mind. Talking to the counselors – Patricia Rodriguez, Susan Cottle-Gooden, Mr. Mims – you get a way to focus, getting your mind straight and body straight. They help you get up on your feet. They will give you strength enough to walk. They give it to you straight." For Marshall, "You may not get well [right away], but the healing starts here. You can't get that anywhere else. They won't run out on you, and you get the psychological part. You will be accepted; they show you here that they care."

Every day it is an honor for me to work alongside our CHC and ISPA clinicians who, in addition to mastering the sciences of healing, have mastered the art of caring.

Dr. Paul
March 26, 2009

Abandon isolation all who enter here; we offer you community.

If, as Mother Teresa teaches us, "loneliness and the feeling of being unwanted is the most terrible poverty," then many of the persons who live on the streets of Miami are doubly poor. Until they come to Camillus House, that is.

There are many causes of isolation.

Many persons who live on the streets suffer serious mental illnesses that leave them helplessly trapped in a world of imaginary friends or unrelenting tormenters. Their isolation is truly tragic. For those with few psychiatric problems, many factors contribute to their isolation and resultant loneliness.

Some choose isolation to minimize their shame at being homeless. "You isolate yourself a lot, you feel ashamed," William admits, "You go in your shell. You don't want people to help you. You stay alone, covered up." Others stay away even from other persons who are homeless to avoid being taken advantage of or to minimize the likelihood of arrest. "I never ask anybody for anything," Harcourt says. "When you're by yourself, you stay out of trouble. When police see a lot of homeless people, they want to hassle you." William echoes these sentiments: "There are less problems when you are alone. And, the addiction takes you into a society of not being in society."

Yet most crave even the slightest acknowledgement from the persons they encounter everyday – a nod, a smile, a kind word – but are ignored by pedestrians and motorists who act as if they do not exist.. "I feel rejected," Angel shares, "I decided to spend time alone to not feel rejected. I start feeling lonely." "You're isolated, and fearful for your well-being," Chechy adds, "You're an outcast."

Regardless of the cause (with the possible exception of those who are seriously mentally ill), the effect of isolation tends to be the same for all: an enveloping sense of loneliness. William says that he becomes lonely for affection and family…and attention: "You want to be able to love somebody. When you find somebody to take time out and listen, that brings you up." All are eager to engage the people they encounter on the street. "You try to find a way to relate, to communicate, says Angel. "They think you want something from them. Sometimes all you want is some human contact." All agree. Like persons who are one paycheck away from homelessness, for many persons already homeless, they are one friend away from loneliness.

Availability, hospitality and respect for all.

Many people find that friend at Camillus House. "They treat you like a family at Camillus House," says Harcourt, "It's togetherness here. When you're sleeping, you don't have to look over your shoulder. You're not lonely any more." Chechy says that "You feel welcome, secure." Staff adds to that sense of togetherness by their

Clients of Camillus House are always welcomed with compassionate hospitality by staff and volunteers.

(Photograph by Gina Fontana)

non-judgmental availability: "You can go to anyone and they answer. We can talk about things here that we wouldn't share on the street," William says. Angel agrees: "Everybody can relate here."

More than friendship, Camillus House offers community. William says that, "There's togetherness here. When we have to go someplace, we go as a group." When asked why she felt that Camillus House offered *her* community, Chechy answered profoundly, "Because I am here." In the end, it is the availability, hospitality and respect shown everyone by the Brothers of the Good Shepherd and our staff that demonstrates to all that Camillus House is a community. It is the guest or client – the stranger – once homeless, who completes for us the guest-host community that is Camillus House. In our March 10, 2005 letter we addressed the power of the guest-host relationship as described by Henri Nouwen:

> In our world full of strangers, estranged from their own past, culture and country, from their neighbors, friends and family, from their deepest self and their God, we witness a painful search for a hospitable place where life can be lived without fear and where community can be found.[29]

Chechy knows that Camillus House is a hospitable place where life can be lived without fear and where community can be found. And, in her words, she knows it, "Because I am here."

Dr. Paul
April 2, 2009

Embrace hope, embrace dignity, embrace healing, for you are in the embrace of your community.

This Lent we investigated whether Camillus House offers hope, dignity, healing and community to persons who are poor and homeless in Miami. The promise of these gifts constitutes the *Camillus Welcome*, displayed on a plaque outside the entrance to the Camillus Courtyard at our main shelter. To help us answer this question, Camillus COO Pat Cawley and I have been meeting over lunch with some of our guests and clients: Marshall, Ivan, William, Mike, Angel, Harcourt and Chechy. I am grateful to them for their thoughtful and honest responses to our inquiries.

"This is what you do."

During our lunches together, our companions told us in a clear and common voice what it means to be at Camillus House. Perhaps the most important aspects of being in our Courtyard are the feeling of security and the experience of unconditional respect. Separation from the chaos and temptations always present on the street – the feeling of security – allows men and women who had survived on the street to begin living a life of self control and self esteem. Then there is the caring shown by all staff; who, professionally trained or not, all participate in the physical, mental and spiritual healing work of Camillus House. Recall Henri Nouwen's words (see my *Letter* of March 10, 2005):

> Healing is the humble but also very demanding task of creating and offering a friendly empty space where strangers can reflect on

their pain and suffering without fear, and find the confidence that makes them look for new ways right in the center of their confusion...[30] The real host is the one who offers that space where we do not have to be afraid and where we can listen to our own inner voices and find our own personal way of becoming human.[31]

Last week, Miami Archbishop John C. Favalora visited the Camillus House main shelter and its Courtyard, accompanied by Archdiocesan Chancellor Msgr. Michael Souckar. As the Archbishop prepared to leave after an extended tour, he glanced at the *Camillus Welcome* plaque. Running his eyes across the words, he said, "Hope, dignity, healing, community...that is what you do." The Archbishop's distinction is important: more than merely *offer* these gifts to persons who are homeless in Miami, he and our luncheon guests have told us that we make hope, dignity, healing and community a living reality in the "friendly empty space" of Camillus House.

Msgr. Michael Souckar,
Miami Archbishop John C. Favalora,
Dr. Paul R. Ahr, and Bob Dickinson

(Photograph by Gina Fontana)

One final sign of the community that is Camillus House can be found in the way clients and staff members treat each other. Today, two of our employees are gravely ill. Victoria Robinson has worked for about 15 months at Mother Seton Village in Homestead. Joe Hodges, who was a member of Camillus' original C.H.A.N.G.E. group of the late 1980s (a forerunner of our ISPA treatment program), has worked for Camillus House for more than 10 years. We pray for them and their families daily. Joe supervises the direct care staff at our Courtyard and Fred Mims tells me that most of the staff at our main shelter and even some clients have visited Joe in the hospital, and that many more clients are praying for his recovery. According to Fred, the Courtyard guests and clients miss Joe's gentle and respectful way with all whom he touches, as do we. Joe and Victoria are part of our Camillus family and we care deeply about them and for them.

Signs and plaques here call out "Welcome!"

As we come to the end of another Lenten season together, I am reminded of the words of Jean Vanier, which we quoted in the last letter of Lent 2005: "Welcome is one of the signs that a community is alive. To invite others to live with us is a sign that we aren't afraid, that we have a treasure of truth and of peace to share." Those who are our guests and visitors tell us that we have such a treasure of truth and of peace to share, and that we share it with all.

When we relocate from the site established by Brother Mathias Barrett, BGS in 1960 to the new Camillus House in 2010, we will leave most of the physical aspects of this Camillus House behind. We will bring with us the *charisms*, or special gifts, of the Brothers of the Good Shepherd: availability, hospitality, flexibility, adaptability and respect for human dignity; and we will bring our guests and clients; our volunteers and staff; our traditions and standards; our appreciation for our benefactors and our love for the poor. We will also bring with us the *Camillus Welcome* plaque as an invitation to persons who are poor and homeless in Miami-Dade County to join us and a promise of what they can expect to experience in the embrace of the Camillus community.

Dr. Paul
April 9, 2009

CHAPTER 9

Advent 2009: Hope, Dignity, Healing and Community

A series of reflections prepared
as we made ready the coming of the
Camillus House Jubilee year

Advent 2009: HOPE

All the great spiritual leaders in history were people of hope. Abraham, Moses, Ruth, Mary, Jesus, Rumi, Gandhi, and Dorothy Day all lived with a promise in their hearts that guided them toward the future without the need to know exactly what it would look like. Let's live with hope.[32] *– Henri Nouwen*

"Advent is a season of hope," Monsignor John Vaughan told his parishioners at St. Patrick's Church on the Beach this Sunday. It is a time of anticipation and preparation. It is an opportunity to practice patient waiting. It is a way to identify with others who are also in waiting.

Why *practice*? In this fast-moving world of ours a high value is placed on spontaneous action, on "getting it right" the first time, rather than on practice making perfect. But as Malcolm Gladwell points out in *Outliers*, those persons whom most would consider the "greatest" in their fields, from technology to business to the arts, have been persons who have practiced and practiced and practiced their skill or art or profession.

Why *patient*? In *Out of Solitude*, Nouwen teaches us that "Without patience our expectation degenerates into wishful thinking. Patience comes from the word *patior* which means to suffer. ...What seems a hindrance becomes a way; what seems an obstacle becomes a door; what seems a misfit becomes a cornerstone." [33]

Why *waiting*? The French authoress Simone Weil writes in her notebook, "Waiting patiently in expectation is the foundation of the spiritual life." [34] Waiting patiently provides the foundation for receptivity and openness.

Over the past several years, the Brothers, Board, benefactors, clients and staff of Camillus House have been practicing patient waiting for the opportunity to begin the work on our new Camillus House campus. Recent events have made the realization of this expectation (not wishful thinking) seem especially elusive. As my wife Pat asks when we are beset by a personal or family setback: "What is the lesson we are supposed to learn here?"

Perhaps the lesson here is to remain one in solidarity with others who are also waiting to achieve their goals, especially the persons we meet at Camillus House who are limited – perhaps even constrained – by their medical conditions, their mental illnesses and addictions, their illiteracy and inadequate education, and their unemployability and poverty. With true compassion for those whom we serve, we – they and us – will prevail as "what seems a hindrance becomes a way; what seems an obstacle becomes a door; what seems a misfit becomes a cornerstone."

Let us live with hope.

Dr. Paul
December 2, 2009

Advent 2009: DIGNITY

> *Paul says, "God has composed the body so that greater dignity is given to the parts which were without it, and so that there may not be disagreements inside the body but each part may be equally concerned for all the others" (1 Corinthians 12:24-25). This is the true vision. The poor are given to the Church so that the Church as the body of Christ can be and remain a place of mutual concern, love, and peace."[35] – Henri Nouwen*

"What child is this, who, laid to rest on Mary's lap, is sleeping? Whom angels greet with anthems sweet, while shepherds watch are keeping?" asks the Christmas anthem. This is the Son of our God who provided for the dignity of all of us so that we may be equally concerned for the welfare of each other. This is Christ who taught us through the *Parable of the Good Shepherd* that through his compassionate availability to a victimized stranger – that is, by *acting on* his feelings of concern, love and peace for another person – the good Samaritan validated the dignity of that stranger, and in doing so, observed the greatest commandment to *love one another*.

When treating all persons with dignity is the work of God Himself, how can we resist doing it? As Pope John Paul II instructed us with regard to the wounded stranger in the Good Samaritan parable, "We are not allowed to pass by on the other side indifferently; we must stop beside him."[36] So, too, we are not allowed to stand by while others are deprived of their inherent human dignity.

Happily, one of the great paradoxes of sharing respect is that when we respect the dignity of another, we elevate the dignity of both that person and ourselves. This is our inherent reward for carrying out the work of God. Consider these remarks that have been attributed to Mother Teresa of Calcutta:

> At the end of our lives, we will not be judged by how many diplomas we have received, how much money we have made or how many great things we have done. We will be judged by 'I was hungry and you gave me to eat. I was naked and you clothed me. I was homeless and you took me in.' Hungry not only for bread – but hungry for love. Naked not only for clothing – but naked of human dignity and respect. Homeless not only for want of a room of bricks – but homeless because of rejection. This is Christ in distressing disguise [emphasis added].[37]

Our clients and guests have told us that the unconditional regard and respect shown them by Camillus staff accelerates their transition from the false self-esteem offered by drugs and alcohol, to a more enduring self-esteem based on unveiling each man's and each woman's inherent human dignity. Our other guests and clients who have a physical and/or mental illness or are merely displaced and/or "down on their luck" share in the enhanced self-esteem that is a by-product of that caring. Good food, the opportunity to rest, the presence of others making the same passage from shame to dignity, and the availability of caring staff to guide the way accelerate the journey.

"You put the dignity in us," William, now a graduate of out treatment program, told us. "No," we reply, "we help you find where you misplaced it, and help you put it on." Let no person here be naked of human dignity and respect. Help all find and put on the dignity that is their birthright so that we can truly be known as "a people of mutual concern, love and peace."

Dr. Paul
December 9, 2009

Advent 2009: HEALING

> *From the point of view of a Christian spirituality, it is important to stress that every human being is called upon to be a healer. Although there are many professions asking for special long and arduous training, we can never leave the task of healing to the specialist. In fact, the specialists can only retain their humanity in their work when they see their professions as a form of service which they carry out, not instead of, but as a part of, the whole people of God. We are all healers who can reach out to offer health, and we all are patients in constant need of help.*[38] – *Henri Nouwen*

There is a display case in the lobby of Camillus' Greer Building in downtown Miami. Here you can see replicas of Camillus Health Concern's *Healing Heart Award*, a statue of Jesus raising up a crippled man, and bearing His question to the blind man outside Jericho (Mark 10:51): "What do you want Me to do for you?" The originals of these statues were separately presented to two persons, an attorney and a nurse. Each of them individually demonstrated Christ's willingness to serve persons who are hurt and homeless, and both of them together exemplify Nouwen's challenge to all persons, health care professionals and lay persons alike, to carry out our vocations as healers.

Our clinical staff and volunteers – the physicians, dentists, psychologists, nurses, social workers, counselors and other health care providers – deal directly with the medical and psychological problems of the persons who are hurt and homeless and seek our clinical skills. Their vocations as healers are easy to understand. But what of the others; how are they to be considered "healers?" "The greatest healing therapy is friendship and love," Hubert

Humphrey once told us. Those of us who are not clinicians heal through compassionate availability. For Nouwen,

> Healing is the humble but also very demanding task of creating and offering a friendly empty space where strangers can reflect on their pain and suffering without fear, and find the confidence that makes them look for new ways right in the center of their confusion.[39]

According to the Buddha: "Our sorrows and wounds are healed only when we touch them with compassion." The power of compassionate companionship comes from heeding the greatest commandment, to *love one another*. This is why Nouwen sees what we call *compassionate companionship* as the most important relationship in the life of another who is hurt or suffering:

> When we honestly ask ourselves which persons in our lives mean the most to us, we often find that it is those who, instead of giving advice, solutions, or cures, have chosen rather to share our pain and touch our wounds with a warm and tender hand. The friend who can be silent with us in a moment of despair or confusion, who can stay with us in an hour of grief and bereavement, who can tolerate not knowing, not curing, not healing and face with us the reality of our powerlessness, that is a friend who cares.[40]

"Nobody cares how much you know until they know how much you care," the Shelter Nurse routinely reminds me. Our Camillus guests and clients are constantly surrounded by and supported by non-clinical staff and volunteers who are caring compassionate companions, as well as by clinicians who have mastered both the sciences of healing and the art of caring.

Rejoice in the knowledge that we are all called to be healers!

Dr. Paul
December 16, 2009

Advent 2009: COMMUNITY

> *In our world full of strangers, estranged from their own past, culture and country, from their neighbors, friends and family, from their deepest self and their God, we witness a painful search for a hospitable place where life can be lived without fear and where community can be found...it is possible for men and women and obligatory for Christians to offer an open and hospitable place where strangers can cast off their strangeness and become our fellow human beings.[41] –Henri Nouwen*

While the general – that is, secular – community has been preparing for Santa Claus (*Here comes Santa Claus, here comes Santa Claus, right down Santa Claus Lane...*) in the months since Labor Day, the Christian community has been preparing the way for the Lord (*O come, O come, Emmanuel...*) in these few weeks leading up to Christmas that we know as Advent (or coming).

Every day of the year we prepare the way for the Lord through our efforts to be and make available to others – especially to strangers – a community of compassionate helpers and healers. In doing so we do not expect that Christ will appear as a child left at our 8th Street gate. If He does appear, He will likely come as a stranger to that gate, presenting as, in the words of Mother Teresa, "Christ in distressing disguise." This is why St. Benedict instructed his Monks to "Let all guests who arrive be received as Christ, because He will say: 'I was a stranger and you took Me in.' (Matthew 25:35-40)...Let the greatest care be taken, especially in the reception of the poor and travelers because Christ is received specially in them..."

How do we come to assume the role of hosts to Christ? For most of us – Brothers, Board Members, other benefactors, other volunteers and staff – it is our special calling to respond to the invitation of the gospels to *love one another* as a community of compassionate helpers and healers. We aspire to be the type of community Nouwen describes: one that is not an organization but a *way of life*, where we gather around us people with whom we want to proclaim the truth that we are the beloved sons and daughters of God. Fortified by the charisms of the Brothers of the Good Shepherd – respect for human dignity, availability, hospitality, flexibility and adaptability – and guided by their example, we are a community that is ready and willing to serve persons who are poor and homeless, for our Faith teaches us that one of the ways that Christ makes His presence manifest to us is as a homeless person.

It is good for us to realize that, like the Magi who brought gifts to the Christ Child, we too have made ready our gifts. Like *gold, frankincense*, and *myrrh*, our gifts of hope, dignity, healing and community are of great value. We offer ours to all in Christ's name, all the while hoping that Christ Himself will be our guest, presenting as a stranger.

"O come, O come, Emmanuel" our hospitable place where life can be lived without fear – our community – beckons. Come even in distressing disguise. You can find us, not down Santa Claus Lane, but at the corner of NE 8th Street and NE 1st Avenue in Miami, as well as in the hearts and deeds of the thousands of persons who are our Brothers, Boards, benefactors, volunteers and staff.

Merry Christmas to all!

Dr. Paul
December 23, 2009

NOTES

16.   114   In the Roman Catholic Church, there are three degrees of sanctity. At the highest degree, the person is canonized and is thereafter referred to as *Saint*. Pope John Paul II canonized 482 persons as Saints during his papacy. At the next highest degree, the person is Beatified and referred to as *Blessed*. Pope John Paul proclaimed 1,338 men and women Blessed, bringing them to the last step before sainthood. They include Mother Teresa of Calcutta and Pope John XXIII. The first step on the path toward canonization occurs when a person is proclaimed by the Pope to be a "Servant of God," and is awarded the title of *Venerable*.

17.   116   The quotations in this Chapter are from Pope John Paul II's encyclical *Labor Exercens*.

18.   122   The quotations in this Chapter are from Pope John Paul II's encyclical *Evangelium Vitae*.

19.   125   The quotations in this Chapter are from Pope John Paul II's encyclical *Salvifici Doloris*.

20.   131   The quotations in this Chapter are from Pope John Paul II's encyclical *Dives in Misericordia*.

Chapter 6

21.   142   Pat Cawley is Camillus House's Chief Operating Officer. Kathy Garcia directs Camillus House's Institute of Social and Personal Adjustment (CH-ISPA), the substance abuse and mental illness program of Camillus House.

22.   143   In Pedro "Joe" Greer's *Waking Up in America*, p. 33.

23.   147   In Carol Novato's *Brother Mathias*.

24.   152   In Nouwen's *The Return of the Prodigal Son*, p. 53.

25.   153   *The Return of the Prodigal Son*, p. 54.

26.   156   In Philip Birnbaum's *Encyclopedia of Jewish Concepts*, p. 61.

Chapter 7

27.   173   St. John Neumann (1811-1850) was the first American Bishop to be elevated to Sainthood.

28. 173 Around the year 1200, two religious orders, the Trinitarians and the Order of Our Lady of Ransom, were founded to recover Christian pilgrims who were kidnapped for ransom or sold as slaves. Members of the Order of Our Lady of Ransom took a vow to surrender themselves in place of those whom they were not otherwise able to redeem from slavery.

Chapter 8

29. 202 *Reaching Out*, pp. 65-66.

30. 204 *Reaching Out*, p. 97.

31. 204 *Reaching Out*, p. 102.

Chapter 9

32. 209 In Henri Nouwen's *Bread for the Journey*: January 16.

33. 209 In Henri Nouwen's *Out of Solitude*, p. 55.

34. 210 Quoted in *Out of Solitude*, p. 55.

35. 211 *Bread for the Journey*, October 31.

36. 211 *Salvifici Doloris*, VII, para. 28.

37. 212 Quoted at http://www.maltausa.org/lourdes_2007.php.

38. 213 *Reaching Out*, p. 92.

39. 214 *Reaching Out*, p. 97.

40. 214 *Out of Solitude*, p. 38.

41. 215 *Reaching Out*, p. 65.

BIBLIOGRAPHY

Birnbaum, P. 1975. *Encyclopedia of Jewish Concepts*. New York: Hebrew Publishing Company.

Curtayne, A. 1954. *St. Brigid of Ireland*. New York: Sheed & Ward.

Erickson, E.H. 1950. *Childhood and Society*. New York: W.W. Norton & Company, Inc.

Gladwell, M. 2008. *Outliers: The Story of Success*. New York: Little, Brown and Company.

Greer, P.J., Jr. 1999. *Waking Up In America: How one doctor brings hope to those who need it most*. New York: Touchstone.

Homer 1952. *The Odyssey*. Chicago: Encylcopaedia Britannica.

Lovato, C.N. 1987. *Brother Mathias: Founder of the Little Brothers of the Good Shepherd*. Huntington, IN: Our Sunday Visitor Publishing Division.

Nouwen, H.J.M. 1985. *Bread for the Journey: A Daybook of Wisdom and Faith*. New York: Darton, Longman & Todd, Ltd., and Doubleday.

Nouwen, H.J.M. 1974. *Out of Solitude: Three Meditations on the Christian Life*. Notre Dame, IN: Ave Maria Press, Inc.

Nouwen, H. J. M. 1986. *Reaching Out: The three movements of the spiritual life*. New York: Image Books.

Nouwen, H.J.M. 1992. *The Return of the Prodigal Son: A story of homecoming*. New York: Image Books

O'Donohue, J. 1999. *Eternal Echoes: Exploring our yearning to belong*. New York: Cliff Street Books.

Vanier, J. 1989. *Community and Growth*. Mahwah, NJ: Paulist Press.

ABOUT THE AUTHOR

Since 2004, Dr. Paul R. Ahr has served as president and chief executive officer of Camillus House in Miami, where he provides general oversight of day-to-day operations of this Roman Catholic non-profit organization. Currently celebrating the 50th anniversary of its founding in 1960, Camillus House provides a continuum of services at 14 sites to men, women and children who are poor and/or homeless in Miami-Dade County, FL. Each night, more than 1,000 persons spend the night under a Camillus House roof.

A licensed psychologist with extensive experience in the mental health and rehabilitative treatment fields, Dr. Ahr is a former director of the State of Missouri's Department of Mental Health (1979-1986) and former Assistant Commissioner for the Virginia Department of Mental Health and Mental Retardation (1975-1979). In 1986, he founded the Altenahr Group, Ltd., a management consulting firm with offices in St. Louis, MO and Miami Beach, FL, consulting with over 150 major corporations, not-for-profit organizations and other agencies.

A native of New Jersey, Dr. Ahr was a *cum laude* graduate of the University of Notre Dame. He was awarded a doctorate degree in clinical psychology by the Catholic University of America in Washington, D.C. and a master's degree in public administration from the University of Southern California. He was a post-doctoral fellow in community mental health administration at the Harvard Medical School, was awarded a certificate in international affairs by Washington University in St. Louis and a certificate in spirituality studies by St. Thomas University in Miami Gardens, FL. He has held teaching posts at Boston University, Virginia Commonwealth University, the University of Southern California and the University of Missouri-Columbia.

Dr. Ahr is the author of two books on public mental health services and co-authored a third book, on employee retention, with his son, Dr. Thomas B. Ahr. He is married to Patricia A. Forde, and together they have three additional children, Andrew, Victoria and Patricia, and two grandchildren, Matthew and Brian.

His book, *Letters to Camillus: Autobiography of a Ministry,* and its Spanish language version, *Cartas a Camillus: Autobiografía de un Ministerio,* are available through the Institute of Homeless Studies Press.

ABOUT CAMILLUS HOUSE

Camillus House was founded in August 1960 by Brother Mathias Barrett, BGS to serve Cuban exiles and other poor persons in downtown Miami. Since then, the Camillus House family has grown dramatically from the small rented house where Brother Mathias fed a hungry man a bowl of donated corn flakes and milk. Presently operating at more than a dozen sites throughout Miami-Dade County, the Brothers of the Good Shepherd, Board members, volunteers, and approximately 175 Camillus professional and support staff:

- Provide 450,000 free meals a year.
- Offer free showers, clothing, mail service and social services to men and women who are homeless.
- Operate state-of-the-art treatment facilities for persons who are homeless and who have physical illnesses and mental and substance abuse disorders.
- Offer job training and job placement services to persons who are homeless and out of work.
- Provide emergency, transitional and permanent housing to nearly 1,000 persons each night.

Dedicated to *eliminating chronic homelessness in Miami-Dade County*, Camillus House plans to:

- Replace our existing shelter building with a newer, larger facility designed to meet the needs of persons who are homeless and respect the privacy and security of our new neighbors.

- Expand our physical and behavioral health treatment programs, including doubling the size of our highly effective substance abuse and mental illness treatment programs, especially for women and Spanish-speaking persons.
- Provide classroom and training space for industry-based career development programs.
- Develop new affordable housing for approximately 550 persons in Miami who have a disabling condition and have been homeless for an extended period of time.

For more information on Camillus House visit
www.Camillus.org

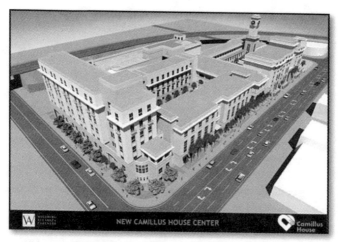

For more information on Camillus' future center visit
www.Camillus-ODH.org